Albert Bennet Whiting

Religion and morality

A criticism on the character of the Jewish Jehovah and the patriarchs

Albert Bennet Whiting

Religion and morality
A criticism on the character of the Jewish Jehovah and the patriarchs

ISBN/EAN: 9783337101732

Printed in Europe, USA, Canada, Australia, Japan

Cover: Foto ©Lupo / pixelio.de

More available books at **www.hansebooks.com**

RELIGION AND MORALITY.

A CRITICISM,

ON THE CHARACTER OF THE

JEWISH JEHOVAH,

THE

PATRIARCHS, PROPHETS, EARLY CHURCH FATHERS, POPES, CARDINALS, PRIESTS, AND LEADING MEN OF CATHOLIC AND PROTESTANT CHURCHES, WITH A DEFENCE OF SPIRITUALISM, &c.

JACKSON, MICH.
T. F. & G. S. BOUTON, PRINTERS.
1860.

Entered according to act of Congress, in the Clerk's Office of the United States Court, for the District of Michigan, in the year 1860.

PREFACE.

In presenting a work of this kind to the public, we are well aware of the prejudices we shall encounter from a large class of minds, who either will not understand us, or are so bound up in their preconceived notions, that facts are of no avail to them, if they conflict with their cherished opinions. We have no apology to offer them for this book, for it contains nothing but facts; but lest we be misunderstood, we would say in this connection, that the first two chapters of this book are not written with a view to ridicule the bible; far from it, for we revere the *truths* of the bible, as much as any one can. Our object is simply to show from the book itself, the true character of some of the persons there described, and that they were not moral men according to the highest modern standard. In our quotations from scripture, we have given the exact language, chapter and verse, so no one can accuse us of unfairness; we have put no *meanings* to these quotations, but have taken them just as they read. In the three chapters that treat of the early church fathers, history of the Popes and other dignitaries of the Church of Rome, the reader will find a curious history of debauchery and crime. Much there is, which is disgusting and revolting, as must necessarily be the case, where such horrid crimes are spoken of. So far as our quotations from history are concerned, we have in those these chapters, the testimony of over fifty different historians of various character, at every period of time, from the first century up to the present one. We have endeavored, as far as possible, to give their exact language, except in a few instances, where we have been obliged to render their modes of expressions more decent. We have endeavored to treat these hideous immoral accounts, of foreign historians (many of whose opinions we have translated expressly for this work,) in as chaste a manner as possible; and we flatter ourselves, that we have succeeded in making the book so it cannot offend the most fastidious taste, (bearing in mind, of course, the delicacy of the subject treated upon. The seventh chapter treats of the various protestant sects, our opinions upon them, and a large number of well authenticated facts, our authority for which is given therein, and in the concluding chapters, our reasons for considering spiritualism productive of a higher toned morality than any other religion. That the work is perfect we do not pretend, for most of it was prepared, while the author was recovering from a severe illness, without at first thinking of having it printed, or at least not until more time for revision and correction had been given; but the urgent solicitations of many friends, have led us to throw it forth to the public gaze; and if it shall afford instruction or gratification to any mind, our aim is answered.

THE AUTHOR

CHAPTER I.

HEBREW MYTHOLOGY, HISTORY OF JEHOVAH, AND HIS PRACTICAL FREELOVEISM; AMORS OF THE SONS OF GOD, ETC., ETC.

The Hebrew nation, like all others, has its peculiar mythology and theory of creation, which is still, to a great extent, held sacred, not only by the Jews, but by many (so called) Christians; though in the last fifty years, since the science of geology has become better understood than in former years, it, like all other extravagant traditions, has been gradually falling into disrepute, and we allude to it at this time because, in the book of Genesis we find the doctrine of freelove plainly and openly taught. Those who look upon that book as the oldest record extant, must admit that the said doctrine is also old, and must be received among the rest, as sacred. Of the story of Adam and Eve, the siren-like wiles of the serpent, who, it seems after all told the truth, for they "did not die the day they ate thereof, but became as gods, knowing good from evil;" which the gods, (Elohim) finally confessed, for said they, "lest he eat also of the tree of life, and live forever, becoming as one of us, let us turn him out of the garden." Even admitting for the moment, this history to be literally true, what is termed the *fall* was the greatest possible blessing that could occur to them, inasmuch as it raised the primeval pair, and after them all mankind, from a life of indolence and ignorance to usefulness and knowledge; of this, we will only make these passing remarks: The Hebrew myth plainly teaches plurality of gods, as all who are familiar with the original tongue are well aware; all who are versed in ancient history, know that in those days all great men were deified; all wonderful and renowned characters were called gods, demi-gods, or the sons of god. It seems that the Hebrew gods had a number of sons, how many, the book fails to inform us; but they plainly show their human origin in the following quotations: "Now the sons of God saw the daughters of men that they were fair," (Gen. 6, 2;) and the union of the two gave birth to a race of giants, who were men of great renown." After all this, in spite of the intermingling with the gods, the world became very wicked, so much so that it made "God repent that he had made man." How much this resembles that portion of the Hindoo Shasters, where it tells of the incarnation of Brahma; of his creations of a female from his own substance; his amours with her; his assuming the forms of various beasts and birds, that he might thereby become the direct father of all things, both beast and human. "The sons of God"—more than one—in spite of all their influence, the world became more and more wicked, so the Lord if he was good himself had to mourn the waywardness of his sons, (like a great many pious parents now-a-days,) who were guilty of a species of freeloveism in wandering away from their paternal abode, and placing their affections on the daughters of men, (world's people). Here then, according to scripture, is the starting point of the freelove doctrine, old almost as the world itself. Being then of such ancient origin, and having such high authority, is it remarkable that it should have been incorporated more or less into every nation, and among all classes of people, especially those concocted with the different church organizations? But if possible, to make it still more firmly established as a part of the life and practice of the church, (not only of that age but of all time,) the example of the Jewish Jehovah, as shown by the Old and New Testament, was directly in support of freelove. Let us look at the facts as there presented—but first, lest we be misunderstood, we will glance at the origin of Jehovah; see if we can find out who and what he is! We would not for a moment insult the God of the universe, whom we adore and worship; whose wondrous beauties are displayed through all life, by for an instant supposing him to be identical with the Jehovah of the Jews. Elohim, spoken of in the few first chapters of Genesis, seem to be an indefinite and mythical class of personages; but after the flood, and still more, after the time of Abraham, the thing assumes a more historical shape; so, in our opinion, the historical portion of scripture commences with Abraham. The person who appeared to him called himself "God Almighty," but we cannot see a particle of proof that he was God of the World, neither does the record assert it; that Abram thought so we have no doubt; but what did this God do to show his *divine* character? He established the cruel and indecent rite of circumcision, and "promised Abram a son," (Genesis 17). This shews plainly that it could not possibly have been the pure and loving father of all, who could thus delight in blood and indecent mutilation, and afterward tempt Abram to offer his son a sacrifice. Suppose some medium should now ascend some one of the beautiful hills of New England, and build an altar, take his only son, and after making all things ready for the slaughter, with knife in hand to deal the fatal blow, some passer by should ask him why do you so? and the answer should be "the spirits told me to." What would be the result? Why, lynch law would be used to bring the unnatural father to a proper sense of his iniquity, or he would be confined as a madman, as he would most richly deserve; not only this, but Spiritualists would be taunted with it for years, as a stain upon *their* philosophy. This God appeared unto the other Patriarchs, and always as a human being; but to Moses he most plainly made himself known in the following language, "I am the God of thy fathers, of Abraham, of Isaac and Jacob; I am that I am;" (Ex. 3. 6, 14;) again,

"I appeared unto Abraham, Isaac and Jacob by name of God Almighty, but by my name Jehovah was I not known unto them;" (Ex. 6, 3.) When he appeared unto Moses, in the burning bush, he does not say I am the God of the world, but "of Abram, Isaac and Jacob," and no doubt he was the spirit of a human being, recognized as a tutelary deity by those persons. In the second quotation he tells his name, which he had before withheld as "Jehovah;" this is from the Chaldaic Yahveh, or Yahouvah, which some say means I am, but others say with a greater show of truth, that it means God of the Mountains, Spirit of the Hills, or High Mountain God. In all his intercourse with Moses he seemed to keep very close to his chosen place of resort, i. e. the hills; he showed himself to Moses many times; "talked with him face to face, as a man talketh with his friend," (Ex. 33, 1, 11;) and at another time placed him in the cleft of a rock and very immodestly exposed his nethermost extremities, v. 23. Now the bible says emphatically in many places, "no man hath seen God at any time; no man can see his face and live, etc.;" therefore it is easily seen that Jehovah was a human spirit, not the Eternal God; furthermore we find him fretful, tyranical, murderous, and even more cruel than Moses; for, said he, (Ex. 32, 9-15,) "I have seen this people, and behold it is a stiff-necked people, now therefore let me alone that my wrath may wax hot against them, that I may consume them, and I will make of thee a great nation. And Moses besought the Lord his God, and said wherefore doth thy wrath wax hot against thy people, which thou hast brought out of the land of Egypt with great power and with a mighty hand? Wherefore should the Egyptians speak and say, for mischief hast thou brought them out, to slay them in the mountains, and to consume them from the face of the earth? Turn from thy fierce wrath, and repent of this evil against thy people; remember Abraham, Isaac and Jacob, to whom thou swarest by thy own self, saying, I will multiply thy seed as the stars of heaven, etc." Now, had it not been for Moses he would have destroyed those people in his fierce outburst of passion; but observe the means used, viz: the Egyptians will slander you if you do so. It is plain then, that Jehovah was affected by human opinions, and that his memory was defective, and he did not recollect what he promised the Patriarchs, or else he meant to add perjury to his other numerous crimes. He finally broke his promise, (Ex. 33, 1-2-3;) would not go with them to the promised land, for fear his wrath would again arise and consume them. The Mosaic Code and the great men of those times will be considered in chapter 2. We will now speak of Jehovah as a freelover; not to mention his officiousness in acting as midwife for Rebecca, Leah, Rachel, etc., (Gen. 25, 21-23; 29, 31-35; 30.) Look at his conduct as recorded in Num. 31; read that chapter and you will find that he commanded them to slay all, old and young, with the exception of the virgins; and of these, as well as of all the other spoil, a part were reserved for him. One might well inquire, what could the Lord want of spoil, of jewels and of cloths, camels, asses, etc.; but what in the name of all that is good and pure could he want of those thirty-two young women, the number that was set apart as his portion? The investigator has no room for conjecture, for the word given by himself before the battle, explains the whole thing in all its horrid details: "Kill all the males, and all the females save those who have not known man; save those alive for yourselves!" This by direct command of this being whom we are taught by the clergy to worship as God. Thirty-two thousand young women were given over to prostitution; this same god reserving for himself thirty-two. Can the human imagination conceive of a worse picture than that? In all the stories of Satan was there ever so black a deed recorded. 'Tis enough to make the angels in heaven weep, and hide their faces with shame, that man should stoop so low as to worship such a being, clothed in the darkest robe of freelove, and recking with spiritual abomination. We will conclude this sketch of Jehovah, by asking one question, predicated on the idea taught by the apostles, (not Jesus,) in regard to his miraculous conception. Now Jesus always called himself the Son of Man, acknowledging Joseph as his father, through whom his genealogy is also traced, and not in a single instance do we find him giving credence by word or deed, to the fabulous statement of his biographers. His code of morals was exalted, he preached against freelove, and denounced priestcraft in all its forms, despised the holy days and ceremonials of the Jews; in short, was a Spiritualist in the highest degree, being guarded by angels through his life, and in the struggles of a cruel and painful death, which he suffered for truth's sake.

If the theory of his birth and parentage as taught by christians generally is correct, we would ask, who was the father of Jesus?

If the reply is "God;" we would then ask who committed adultery with the young wife of Joseph?

According to their version, it would seem that Jesus, the second person in the trinity, was a product of a freelove union between the first person and a young virgin. Why then does the christian world try to shirk the responsibility of the freelove doctrine, when a part of their god owes to it his existence? Oh, consistency, where art thou? thou art not here!

CHAPTER II.

THE CHARACTER OF GOD'S CHOSEN SERVANTS, THE PATRIARCHS, KINGS, PROPHETS, PRIESTS, CHIEFTAINS, JUDGES, WARRIORS, ETC.

One would naturally suppose, and rightfully too, that if an infinite God selected chosen subjects for particular purposes, he would take those who were pure and righteous, and so he would; but in the first place, the Infinite Deity, the Soul of the Universe, of whom the Psalmist seems to have had a very correct idea when he said: "Though I ascend to Heaven, yet He is there; though I make my bed in Hell, yet he is there;" would never stoop to specialities. His general law is long enough, broad enough, deep enough, and minute enough to answer all His high purposes. Then again, if special acts were necessary, He would select a different class of people, with different moral characters, from those we are about to describe. It was shown in Chapter 1st, that the cruel, vindictive monster, worshiped by the Jews and many so-called Christians, is altogether a different person from the God of Nature. We are also well aware that the standard of morality taught and practiced by His chosen people, was in direct accordance with that of their tutelary deity. Those men also were as good, aye, many of them better than the generality of men at that time; that there were many of them mediums, and received high and exalted thoughts from spirits, known to them as angels, gods, etc.; but these spirits were by no means perfect, or more elevated than those who now return to earth; but many of them, judging by their communications, lower than anything of the kind we have in this age. We do not admit these men to be patterns of morality, for us to follow or admire.

First, the Patriarchs, commencing with Abraham, who was particularly favored by this earthly god: of his cruel and insane attempt to sacrifice his only son, we have already spoken. We come now to the freelove part of his life. His first exploit in this department, is found in Gen. 16th, where, by the suggestion of his wife, he takes her servant maid for a concubine; then afterward, this pious woman shamefully abused the wretched victim of her own misguided tastes. He also passed his wife off as a sister once, when traveling in Egypt, "that it might be well with them." She was taken into the house of Pharaoh, for what purpose is not revealed. In another instance, Abraham denied his wife to Abimelech, (Gen. 20); she came very near being made a victim through such denial; in short, it appears he denied her for that very purpose, but some spiritual agent, there called god, came to Abimelech, and told him the facts. It then came out that she was half-sister to Abram, thus proving him guilty of incest, in addition to his other crimes. Abraham lived a great many years, was a man well known and respected, notwithstanding all this. Lot, brother of Abraham, was a very good man, according to the record; he was also a medium, for angels came to him many times, in form of men; on one occasion he made a feast for them, but when the wicked Sodomites gathered around the house, demanding these men to be delivered up to their unnatural passions, what says this righteous man: " Behold now, I have two daughters which have not known men, let me, I pray you, bring them out unto you, and do ye to them as is good in your eyes." This was the only righteous man in Sodom. What would be thought of the father now, who would offer to give up his two virtuous daughters to minister to the depraved passions of a rabble? He would be justly execrated and despised by all good citizens.

If he was the only good man, what in the name of Heaven could the rest have been? In what depths of passion, cowardice and crime must they have dwealt? His acts after he escaped from Sodom, were more disgustingly brutal than those just mentioned; and display his and his daughters' *virtue* in the most unenviable light, and display them as notorious freelovers, and guilty of the double crime of drunkenness and incest. Lot and Abram were brothers, what would they be called, judged by our code of morals? A precious pair of scamps and adulterers, deserving at least of the State Prison.

Jacob, who was afterward called Israel, was another of the chosen ones, a recipient of angelic influences, and yet he commenced his career by cheating his brother out of his birthright, and several other equally dishonorable acts. He procured his two wives in a very remarkable way; he served seven years for one, and his father-in-law cheated him by putting another in her place, and requiring him to serve seven years more, for her he truly loved, (Gen. 29th.) This is his first freelove adventure, taking two wives at once; not satisfied with this, Rachel, because she had no offspring of her own, delivered up her hand maid as a third affinity to Jacob, that she might raise up children for her; she then, in spite of her pretended love for Jacob, for a few mandrakes, consents to deliver her bed to Leah, (Gen. 30, 15). After Leah saw what her sister had done, she followed her example, and gave him her hand maid, so his affinities were again increased, and his progeney also. When he started to leave the mansion of his respected father-in-law, not satisfied with the wealth he had obtained, he must needs by a stratagem, secure a large portion of Laban's flocks, and the best of all both sheep and cattle; and his favorite wife winds up by stealing her father's images, which were no doubt very choice and valuable, then resorted to an immodest stratagem to conceal them from her father when he searched, (Gen.

31, 14–35.) Such then was the code of morals of these chosen ones of deity. Jacob, of whom it was said, "he wrestled with god, and overcame him." What kind of a being must it have been, who would associate intimately with such a man as we have shown Jacob to be? A great financier, but a cheat, swindler, and freelover. His sons and daughters, most of them, were but little better than himself, in this respect. Reuben, his eldest, was guilty of immoral practices, and breach of trust besides, (Gen. 35, 22.) The adventures of Shechem and Dinah, as recorded in Gen. 34th, and the treachery of Jacob's sons in dealing with the former, show the Hebrew character in its true light, better than any remarks we can make. The conduct of the ten toward the unoffending Joseph, by far the best of the twelve, shows the dark chicanery which they justly inherited from their parents. He was a moral man, even rejecting the most seductive advances of Potiphar's wife, (Gen. 34, 7–9). In Gen. 38, we find a tale of freeloveism, of most disgusting form, together with other numerous crimes. Judah, one of the twelve, gets very much disappointed, for what he supposed to be an harlot, proved to be his daughter in-law, Tamar, who had twins by him. The rest of the chapter is too vulgar to be quoted; it adds another page to the dark catalogue of Hebrew immoralities.

Moses, the great Lawgiver of the Jews, and their leader out of Egyptian bondage, was of humble origin; he was found in an ark floating in the bulrushes, by a servant girl of Pharaoh's daughter, by whom he was adopted. He signalized himself by a murder, when he was quite a young man, and hid his victim's body in the sand, (Ex. 2, 12,) then fled into the land of Midian, where he was taken into favor by the high priest, who gave him his daughter Zipporah to wife; it was there, on Mount Horeb, that he had his first introduction to Jehovah, the Spirit of the Mountains, who appeared to him in a burning bush, with certain revelations, and among other things, commanded him to rob the Egyptians; more than that, for all the women of Israel to be instructed to steal all they could, and assist in the work of spoliation, (Ex. 3–22). No wonder Zipporah called him "a bloody husband," [Ex. 4, 25–26,) for even the idolatrous Midianites had nothing in their rites so horrible as circumcision. We pass over a great many wonderful events in the life of Moses, who undoubtedly in some respects, was the greatest man of that age; he instituted a great many laws that were no doubt beneficial and necessary; but the extreme vulgarity of the whole Levitical Code, shows the depraved state of the people he had to govern. He shows the darkest phase of his character in Numbers, 31, where he goes forth to spoil Midian, the country of his father-in-law; he sent forth his armies by command of Jehovah, to destroy that unoffending nation, [because, forsooth, they did not bow down before the High Mountain God,] with the strict injunction to slay all, except the virgins. Here then, we find him, in connection with Eleazar the priest, under the guidance of Jehoveh, assisting in the prostitution of thirty-two thousand virtuous women. Even this great man Moses, was a freelover on a scale so large that we moderns tremble while gazing upon the record; what then must have been the awful reality? We find Moses then a murderer, thief, robber and adulterer. He, the chosen one to lead the children of Israel out of bondage; not only this, but we find the doctrine of free-love plainly taught by him in Deut. 24, [notwithstanding his previous denunciations in Leviticus,] in the following language: "When a man hath taken a wife, and it come to pass she find no favor in his eyes, let him write her a bill of divorcement, and send her out of his house, then she may go and be another man's wife." If that is not freelove in its most radical sense, what is it? This much for the oracle of the Hebrew Nation, so righteous that his guardian spirit took him away privately after his death, "so it was not known where his body was lain," and children are to-day in Sunday schools taught that he was such a good and meek man, that God buried him.

Joshua, the next chosen one of Jehovah, was a great warrior, brave and bloodthirsty, just the man for the times, we admit. But the very first thing he did on entering Jerico, was to seek out a harlot, at whose house his two spies lodged; and the only ones deemed worthy of being saved after the destruction of the city, were this same harlot, Rahab, and her household, [Josh. 2, 6.] He also re-established the old rite of circumcision, instituted by Abram. The whole

Book of Joshua, is but a record of bloodshed and crime. We pass over this book, and Judges, after noting one or two characters in the latter. Samson stands out as the most wonderful man of that book; the man of prodigious strength, whose remarkable deeds of valor eclipsed the accounts of the heathen gods, whose battles were many, and performances with foxes, are as familiar as household words, (how those three hundred foxes must have looked, running with their tails all ablaze,) throughout Christendom. Even this strong man was captivated by a harlot, and given over to the Philistines; so his exceeding great passion was the means of his captivity and death; he, the mighty Samson, conquered by the festering wiles of a designing woman. In Judges 19th, we find a horrible account of the immorality and cruelty of a Levite; now the Levites were the highest order of priesthood, who according to the Jewish Code, were required to be better than the rest of mankind, and patterns of morality, yet this one had a concubine, who it appears got tired of him, and went away to her father's house; was gone for months; the priest got lonesome and went after her to speak friendly to her, and bring her back again; he arrived at the house of her father, who was glad to see him, so much so, that he kept prolonging his stay, till he remained several days; then started for home with the woman; on their way they stopped at a certain city to stay over night, and certain men of Belial got around, demanding that he should be given up to them. No! said the host, I will give you my daughter and his concubine, do with them as you please. This was done, and the poor concubine, after being left by the rabble, managed to crawl up to the threshold, and lay there till morning. The worst part of the story is yet to come: one would suppose that this pious Levite, on finding her there, would take her up tenderly and give her proper medical treatment; instead, he spake out sharply, saying: "up, and let's be going!" Finding she answered not, he took her up, carried her home, and cut her into twelve pieces, dividing even the bones, and sent a piece to each of the twelve tribes of Isrel. Is there anything in paganism that equals this act, for the very essence of cruelty and barbarous treatment? If there is, or was, we have yet to see it in print. And the perpetrator of this atrocious deed was a member of the highest order of priesthood; verily, Jehovah chose strange servants to minister in his sanctuary. The story of Ruth contains within itself a singular and interesting account of the state of morals at that time; but to bring it down to modern times and language, suppose some managing mamma should direct her only remaining daughter, whom she was anxious to marry off to good advantage, to wash herself, fix up in her best attire, annoint her body with perfumes; then after arranging her dress to show off in the best possible manner, in the most bewitching style to captivate, and then go and lie down on the floor near where a man was winnowing grain; she being charged to wait till he had done his work and eaten and drunken, till he was excited or stupefied with wine; then to lie down beside him, (after he had lain down) and cover herself up with his blanket. He, awakening after the effects of the wine had subsided, would no doubt be quite surprised to find a young woman beside him, he being a man somewhat advanced in years, and if he was anything of a gallant, he would be very apt to compliment her on her preference, and praise her for not running after young men, either rich or poor; and would, no doubt, being subject to human weakness, and heated by wine, promise to do all she required. Such is the story of Ruth, brought down to modern modes of expression; it is found mostly in Chapter 3d, of that interesting book. It appears moreover, after this adventure, that Boaz was so well pleased with his sleeping companion, he concluded to marry her; so the husband seeking daughter and the managing mamma, were both successful in the attainment of their desires. What would the world think of such conduct to-day? It would be justly condemned in all good society; and the woman who got a husband in that way would always be subject to reproach. Such acts, when they do occur, are trumpeted thro' the press as a *new development* of freelove; an appropriate term to be sure, but rather ancient in its significance.

We are aware Theologians and Commentators try to gloss over this and other immoral stories in the Bible; but it will not answer; people will think for themselves, or at least, some will.

The Prophet Samuel was a great man, and a medium also, and

tho' he commanded some very cruel acts in his life, his general character was better than most men of that country. He was ahead of the times in a great many respects. One dark blot upon his character was the slaying of Agag, the captive King of Amelek. After he had got him in his power, he hewed him in pieces in cool blood, out of pure revenge, (1st Samuel 15, 32-35). He caused Saul to be proclaimed King, but because he was not sufficiently active in carrying out his commands, or those of his guardian spirit, (the same Jehovah that directed Moses,) he was deposed, and David made King in his place, David was a very "handsome man and goodly to look upon," a great harpist, he played once before Saul, to drive away an evil spirit, and was successful. " So wonderful wos his playing, that he charmed all who listened to his music," 1st Samuel, 16, 15-23. He was also endowed with powerful strength, and skill at war; slew the giant Goliath, Chief of the Philistines, with a single stone. But let us inquire into his morals. He was a great favorite with the ladies, who sang his praises in the following language, accompanying themselves on various instruments: "And it came to pass as they came when David was returned from the slaughter of the Philistines, that the women came out of all the cities of Israel, to meet King Saul, singing and dancing, with tabrets, with joy, and with instruments of music. And the women answered one another as they played, and said, Saul hath slain his thousands, but David his tens of thousands," (1 Samuel, 17, 6-7.)" This naturaally made Saul jealous, and he sought to kill David, but failed in the attempt; the latter fell in love with Saul's daughter, who returned the passion. The young lady's father would not give his consent unless David would comply with a very extravagant, indecent and cruel request, involving the mutilation of an hundred Philistines, (1 Sam. 18, 25-28. This did not daunt the young man at all, he was rather pleased with this chance to display his skill; so he brings twice the number required, torturing two hundred instead of one, and on his return received Michal, daughter of Saul, as his reward. This was his first love adventure. The next, we find in the 25th chapter of the same book. Here, a woman, Abigail is represented as coming to David, and after humbling herself in the dust, and professing for him all manner of reverence, goes on to tell what a Nabal [old fool] her husband is, by name and nature; imploring the King that when the Lord did well by him, he would remember her. David said unto her "go up in peace, for I have hearkened unto thy voice, and received thy person." Soon after, by some mysterious process, her husband was put to death; and immediately the King sent for her to be his second wife. About the same time he took a third one, called Ahinoam; then winds up this chapter by allowing his first wife, Michol, (whom he had probably tired of by this time,) to be given away to Phaiti, the son of Laish. David was a great singer and dancer. He paid tribute to the memory of Saul in a very beautiful song, accompanying himself on the harp. He afterwards made a sort of ark, around which he danced in the presence of all Israel, with nothing round him but a linen ephod [girdle]. His conduct on this occasion so shocked Michal [Saul's daughter,] that she reproved him for thus uncovering himself, like a foolish fellow. David was very wroth, and consoled her by saying: "I will be yet more vile than this, and will be base even in mine own sight, and of the maid servants which thou hast spoken, of them shall I be had in honor. So Michal had no children to the day of her death, because she had thus rebuked her King," [2 Sam. 6, 16–23]. His next free-love adventure is found in 2d Samuel, 11. He sees the beautiful Bathsheba, and his passion for her becomes ungovernable; he sent for her in the absence of her husband; she, nothing loth, became his fourth affinity. But the villain, not yet content, after entertaining her husband Uriah, under show of friendship, he wrote his death warrant, put it in his own hands to take to the commander in chief of the army; he was slain, and just as soon as his wife was done with the show of mourning, David sent for her again, and she became his. This villainous deed displeased even his tutelary God. After he had become an old man and stricken in years, his ruling passion was still strong, although his physical powers were inadequate to fill that passion's demand. They must needs send a great distance for one Abishag, a Shunamite, a beautiful young lady, to try to rouse the decayed energies of the now impotent King; but it was useless, "for the King knew her not," [1 Kings, 1, 1-4]. All their arts were unavailing, and David, the mighty King of Israel was on his deathbed. No more to sound the **Harp** or strike the Timbrel; no more to lead armies forward, conquering and to conquer; no more to revel in luxurious freelove and freelove delights; no **more to dance naked before the Lord.** One would think such a man on his deathbed, would repent of some of his evil deeds; if **he did, he performed then and there, if possible**, still darker ones than ever before. In his dying charge to his favorite son, Solomon, (1 Kings, 2, 8-10,) he speaks as follows:

"And behold **thou hast with thee** Shimei, the son of Gera, a Benjamite of Bahurim, which cursed me with a grievous curse, in the day I went to Mohanaim, but he came down to meet me at Jordan, and I sware to him the Lord, saying, I will not put thee to death with the sword. Now therefore, *hold him not guiltless;* for thou art a wise man and knowest what thou oughtest to do unto him, *but his hoar head bring thou down to the grave with blood!*" So David slept with his fathers, and was buried in the city of kings.

So, the death of poor old Shimei, was the thing nearest the heart of **the** King on his deathbed: and the last words of this holy man, were: "*Bring his hoar head down to the grave in blood!*" This was the "man after God's own heart, who sinned not, save in the matter of Uriah, the **Hitite**." His last act, instead of being one of mercy, was cold blooded revenge.

The sons of David were, most of them, very much like their father, so far as freelove was concerned. Ammon became enamored of his half-sister, Tamar, and by feigning himself sick, was enabled to commit the double crime of ravishment and incest. (2 Sam. 13.) Absalom was a very beautiful man, and a "long haired champion" besides, as it seems from the weight of hair he polled yearly, (2. Sam. 14. 25-26). He was a usurper, stole the hearts of Israel, and tried to dethrone his father; and on one occasion, by counsel of a confidential friend, he went in on a large scale, as follows: "And Ahithopel said unto Absalom, go in unto thy father's concubines, which he hath left **to keep the house.** So they spread Absalom a tent upon the top of the house: and Absalom went in unto his father's concubines in the presence and sight of all Israel. And the counsel of Ahithopel, was as if a man had inquired at the Oracle of God." Absalom finally met with a violent death, and his father mourned for him as a favorite son. He was truly, after modern expression, a chip of the old block.

Solomon, son of David, by Bethsheba, was chosen to succeed his father as King of Israel. He is represented as the wisest man that ever lived. He may have been the wisest man that had ever then lived, but to call him the best that ever should life, is simply absurd. He was a great King, and with the assistance of pagan artisans from Tyre, built a magnificent temple. But was he perfect? By no means, as the history distinctly shows. "For he loved many strange women of almost every Nation on the face of the earth. And he had seven hundred wives, princesses, and three hundred concubines; and his wives turned away his heart. (1 Kings, 11, 1–3).

Here is freeloveism on a scale that Joe Smith and Brigham Young in their palmiest days, never even dreamed of being able to practice. His songs, which are headed as a description of the graces of Christ and the Church, by theological translators, contain not a single word, from beginning to end, that can even be distorted into an account of Chr st or Church. They are merely a collection of amorous effusions, addressed to different females, and couched in language so indelicate, that if a modern author were to write poems in a similar strain, he would be liable to prosecution, and those who almost adore Solomon, would be first to cry him down, and bring him to condign punishment. No wonder he cried in his old age: "Vanity of vanities! all is vanity and vexation of spirit," [Ecc. 1st.]

Any debauchee, after spending a life in illicit love and dissipation, when too late to escape the penalty of his sins, would cry out with sorrow at a life thus misspent. David and Solomon were wise and intelligent men in some respects, we admit; but very great roues, according to our reading of their history.

We leave the minor Kings of Israel, after Solomon, as there is neither time nor space, to consider them all in detail. Moses, David and Solomon are the Hebrew characters most looked up to and quoted by the Christian world. Having shown them up in their true light, we are willing to let the lesser oracles rest till a more convenient season.

Next in order the Prophets. Oh! says the Christian, they were all exemplary men, especially chosen of God to tell future events, of Jesus, etc. Were not some of them freelovers? we enquire. O, no! says the horrified churchman. Did any of them go naked? again we ask. As a general thing they will call us blasphemers, or something worse. But let us see. Isaiah taught a great many beautiful truths, and in the first chapter condemns the idolatry of the Jews in very decisive words of warning, even their holy days and solemn meetings; but we war not with the truth he taught, but would try to find out what kind of a man he was. He and the Lord did a great many very strange things, to say the least. God, thro' Isaiah, threatened to serve a lot of women in rather a scandalous manner, "despoil them of all their garlands, jewels and cloths, and expose their persons in a very indecent way, (Is. 3–17." Whether he was a believer in people generally going naked, he does not inform us, but he certainly went naked himself three whole years, by command of the Lord, as was asserted for a sign, that two whole nations would go naked, even to the most indecent exposure of their whole persons, (Is. 20.) Whether he believed in dark circles or not, he does not say in as many words, but from the curious request he made of a young daughter of Babylon, one would infer such was the case. He spoke to her as follows: "Come down and sit in the dust, oh! virgin daughter of Babylon; sit on the ground, there is no throne, O, daughter of the Chaldeans; for thou shalt no more be called tender and delicate; take the millstones and grind meal, uncover thy lock, make bare thy legs, uncover thy thighs, and pass over the river. Thy nakedness shall be uncovered, yea, thy shame shall be seen; I will take revenge and I will not meet thee as a man; sit thou silent, and get thee into darkness, etc. [Is. 47, 1–5]. Whether she obeyed him, and if so, if he kept his promise, the writer has neglected to inform us. What if a modern medium, under professed spirit directions, should attempt to go naked, after the manner of Isaiah, saying the spirits or the Lord told him to. He would not be allowed to go naked three hours, in any civilized community; and it would be right to restrain such an one; but if it is not allowable now, why should it be excusable in Isaiah, who was a Prophet of the Lord, and as such, ought to have been nearer perfect than other men? Or if a medium should talk to a young lady as he is represented as doing to the one referred to, what would be done with him? And what would be thought of the young woman who would believe such questionable protestations? These are knotty questions for Bible worshipers to solve; especially those who are ever ready to slander their fellow beings, for a difference of opinion.

Jeremiah was a very sad man, is generally known as the weeping prophet. The book bearing his name is full of assertions that will not bear the test of investigation; and extravagant figures of speech some of which are very low and indecent. "Whoredoms, divorces, adulteries, etc.," are his principal types for the different kingdoms whose conditions he portrayed. In chapter 3d, he represents the Lord as being married, and divorced, and married again. Even after a whole nation had become so bad as to commit adultery with stones and stocks, the Lord, speaking through Jeremiah, was then willing to receive them back to their former loves. In the 14th chapter he turns against the Lord, accuses him of deceiving the whole nation; in the 5th he turns upon the people, accuses them all of being adulterous, and each of them neighing after their neighbor's wives; which condemnation was no doubt richly deserved. For what else could be expected of a nation, than that it would pattern after its God and its holy men. Chapter 8, verses 1-2, deals in an awful condemnation of Judah; commanding even that the bones of the people should be desecrated, "lay as dung upon the face of the earth." Verse 10 teaches practical freeloveism, "therefore will I give their wives unto others, etc." In the 20th he again accuses the Lord of deceiving him, turns traitor to the Jews, assisting the Babylonians, and counseled the people to succumb to the Chaldeans. Chapter 23 deals out terrible anathemas against both Prophet and Priest, himself included. In Chapter 25, he and the Lord commanded awful things; verse 27: "Therefore thou shalt say unto them, thus saith the Lord of Hosts, the God of Israel: drink you and be drunken, and spue, and fall, and rise no more. And it shall be if they refuse to take the cup, at thy hand to drink, then shalt thou say unto them, thus saith the Lord of Hosts, ye shall certainly drink." He is deemed a dangerous man by the Priests, Princes and Rulers, is arrested and condemned to death. Finally he made friends with them, and his life was spared, (Chap. 26) So, through all his life, sometimes on one side, again on the other, alternately successful and unsuccessful; and in his lamentations, he lays it all to the Lord, whom he accuses of all manner of evil, and deception; "of throwing sand in his eyes, gravel stones in his teeth," etc. We do not read that he was a freelover himself, but he commended it in others, as will be seen from our quotations.

Ezekiel was the oddest and most vulgar of all the Old Testament Prophets. We doubt if there can be found in any language, the equal of some chapters in that book, for obscenity, and indecent allusions. His first experience in this department is in Chapter 4, where by command of the Lord, he was to lie on his side three hundred and ninety days, and eat of a kind of food horrible to think of, and too vulgar to mention. No wonder he cried, "Ah! Lord God!" when the word was given him. By entreaties, he finally made this Lord God compromise the matter, and make his food a trifle less vile, (seeing he had got to feed on it so long). In Chapter 5, he portrays this Lord in the most terrible form. He there goes so far as to command canibalism. "The fathers shall eat their sons, and the sons shall eat their fathers. Mine eye shall not spare, neither will I have any pity." Chapter 13 deals out wrath against all the rest of the Prophets and Prophetesses, saying wo! wo! threatening to tear the handkerchiefs off their heads, tear their pillows to pieces, and other equally ridiculous performances, all threatened in the name of the Lord. Chapter 15, though called a type of Jerusalem, talks of nothing but whores, whoredom and nakedness, in the most immodest language possible. But by far the most vulgar, immoral and improbable story in the whole Bible, is Chapter 23, where two women, Aholah and Aholiboth are spokin of as a type of Jerusalem and Samaria. Though commentators may try to pass it off as a type of kingdoms, they cannot take a single jot from its innate vulgarity. Were it not too gross for an intelligent public to read, we could show it up in a light that would make the very name of Ezekiel stand synonymous with lewdness and vulgarity. God is represented as having kept these two women for years, even after they had played the harlot with differant nations, and after he cast them off, they extended their amours even into the brute creation Oh! horrid depth of darkness! Is there anything in modern times, in the freeloveism of to-day, that begins to compare with this? No! Not even the grossest obscene books that are tabooed by all virtuous society, and their publishers made amenable to the laws, do we learn of anything that begins with the 23d chapter of Ezekiel. And this man, Ezekiel, who recorded such stuff, was one of the greater Prophets; one of the chosen ones of that time to proclaim the will of the Lord God to mankind.

Daniel was a good man, superior to all the other Prophets in mediumship, morality, and the general correctness of his sayings; he recognized the spiritual influences that governed him, in their true character, viz: angels, or spirits of men that appeared to him. We find more morality in his experiences, than in those of his predecessors, which shows that he had a better idea of the guardian spirits about him, which was no doubt the reason of his being a better man, and more choice in his modes of expression. Hosea goes on something after the manner of Isaiah, threatening to strip people naked, both men and women, and shamefully expose them; and talks extravagantly about making covenants with beasts, fowls, etc., (Hosea 2,1-10) In Chapter 3, he tells about his "falling in love with a harlot, or adulteress, and buying her for fifteen pieces of silver, and for a homer of barley, and half a homer of barley." It appears he bought her for many days. His whole record shows him familiar with that kind of life, for he gives forth his mottos "as one having a large experience," (Chap. 4, v. 10-11).

We find nothing flagrant in Joel, besides, we find a prophecy in Chapter 2, v. 28-29, which is being strikingly fulfilled at the present time. Amos and Obadiah contain nothing worthy of note.

Next comes the wonderful story of Jonah and the whale, too ridic-

4

ulous for sensible people to believe. The other lesser Prophets that follow, contain nothing relevent to the present subject, until Malachi, the last of the number, who reproves the Priests in a way more expressive than elegant, (Chapter 2, v. 1-4); and winds up his last chapter with the very interesting information, that "there shall come a day that shall burn as an oven, and all the proud, aye, and all that do wickedly shall be as stubble, etc." Where! Oh! where! then, we ask, will these Prophets be found? whose wickedness, low character, freeloveism and nakedness, we have just been exposing. Verily, if there are any wicked, they are of the number, according to their own confessions. And we have said nothing of them, except what we find admitted in their writings.

CHAPTER III.

A GLANCE AT THE NEW TESTAMENT; EARLY TRADITIONS OF THE CATHOLIC CHURCH; EXTRVAGANT THEORIES; IMMORALITY OF THE EARLY BISHOPS, AND CHURCH FATHERS AND NICOLAITANS; HISTORY OF THE POPES, ETC.

In the New Testament itself, we find but little to uphold the doctrine of freelove. As we remarked in Chapter 1, Jesus was a good and pure man; and if those who are now most strenuous for the recognition of his divinity, would strive to follow his example, the world would be much better than it now is. His immediate disciples were taken from the lowest ranks of society; he associated with publicans and sinners, not as an equal, but to raise them up if possible, and make them truly better. Peter, one of his most intimate friends, was both a liar and coward, denying his master on three different occasions; yet he was a great medium, performed many wonderful cures, said many beautiful things. Paul did not become a disciple, till after the death of Jesus. He was also a great medium, but blended his old Jewish notions with the Gospel of Jesus, and in his writings we find the first great departure from the principles of Christ, and the first corner stone of modern Christianity. His code of morals was also very low, and his standard of female and male purity was lower. He was a bachelor himself, and an ascetic; so of course not a practical freelover. The condemnations, and unnaturally immoral practices which he says God will bring upon a certain class of people, (Rom. 1), show his gross ideas of Deity and his laws; though these practices and views, as we shall **show, were** afterward incorporated into the Church, and dignified as sacred by some of the sainted ones. So, if that had read, "these immoral practices shall be incorporated into the Church, **in the** name of God," it would have been an exact prophesy **of what came to** pass in a few years. His sensual ideas of marriage, **as recorded** in 1st Cor. 7, contains not **only** a vulgar record, but alas! **the received and** cherished opinions of the christian **world, so far as** marriage is concerned, viewing it simply as legalized prostitution; the only reason alleged by Paul, as deemed by him worthy to offer as an excuse for entering into that relation, is "it is better to marry than to burn." Oh, how degrading to all pure affections is such sentiment as that. But we do not propose to criticise at length the New Testa**ment, for modern** Christianity is founded more on the Old than the New. We shall devote this chapter principally **to a consideration of the characters of** the early church fathers, those holy men, unto whom were given in charge the keys of heaven, and the holy records; and inasmuch, as we have in treating the Bible characters kept close to the book itself, so we shall take the same course, taking the admissions of the Catholic Church, with regard to these personages. The Catholic Church is the parent of all modern Christian Churches, the most ancient and powerful, the "great dragon," against which the powers of light must battle; the rest are mere horns upon the head of the beast "which did make war against her." According to traditions, the keys of heaven were delivered up to St. Peter, and he became the first Bishop of Rome. Simon, the magician, also flourished at that time; he had a concubine whom he asserted was the eternal mother, and consequently divine, and whoever believed on her should see eternal life. St. Peter had a contest with this Magician, who, during the combat, was taken up into the air by Diabolus; when Peter invoked the name of Jesus, he fell to the ground, and perished in a most miserable manner. At this time, there was a great dispute in the churches about the doctrine of circumcision. One Corinthus insisted strongly that it should be continued. The apostles concluded to assemble together, and decide this important question. So, according to Catholic history, the first assembly of Christians as a sect, in the first century, was convened for the purpose of deciding whether people should or should not, be thus indecently mutilated; truly, a worthy subject to be first considered by the fathers of the Christian Church; this took place about the year sixty. Peter, just before his death, (which is said to have taken place in sixty-six,) wrote his second epistle, and also severely condemned the Nicolaites, or Nicolitans, a sect of people who flourished at that time, who pretended to be a sort of halfway Christians, named after Nicolas, one of the seven deacons of Jerusalem. They considered the Trinity, the Virgin, Holy Ghost, original sins, etc., holy mysteries, awful and sublime. Thus it appears, they agreed so far with the Christians; but instead of calling the virgin, Mary, they called her the goddess Barbelo, and Jesus they designated by the longer name Jaldabaoth. This sect repudiated marriage, and were a set of freelovers and Sodomites of the grossest and vilest type. Thus, directly under the nose of Peter and Paul, and cotemporary with the earliest Church fathers, was instituted a sect of practical freelovers, who at that day incorporated into their ceremonials, the darkest forms of the most indecent Hebrew immoralities. This sect is alluded to by Peter in his last epistle, by Paul in his first letter to Timothy, Chapter 4, and by John, in Rev. 2d; all of whom severely condemn their practices. They are also mentioned by many of the early Church historians. The question of marriage or no marriage among the priesthood, was a great bone of contention among the priests and Bishops of the second century. Eleutherus the 14th Pope, advocated strongly the continuance of marriage among the Priests; he accused all those who opposed it of being addicted to concubinage and Sodomy; [no doubt he spoke the truth] he justly condemned them for their boasted purity and sanctity above other men. And it were well for some of our modern priests, both Catholic and Protestant, to give heed to these pungent rebukes of pretentiousness and hypocrisy. Victor, who succeeded him, was seduced by the Montonist faction, under Tertulian, who recognized the prophesies of Montanus Maximilla, and Priscilla. Although this is brought against Victor and Testulian, as an accusation, it would seem from history that these persons were real visionists, and recipients of spiritual gifts, as a class superior to many of their accusers. Another sect of Christians flourished about that time, called Valentinians, after Valentine, their founder; who made freelove a practical duty—this sect, led by Blpstrus and Florinus two apostate priests, practiced all manner of impurities, as a duty; and "maintained that no one could attain perfection till he had loved a woman. All of this was before the beginning of the 3d century, during which century there were a great many cruel and vicious rulers, but none other so dark and depraved, so cruel, licentious, and deplorably vindictive, as Commodus, during whose reign, says history, the Christians enjoyed repose and quiet. Indeed, they were the only sect exempt from his cruelties. Look at history a moment, and see what kind of a man he was in whose reign the Christians were so flourishing, and allowed so much peace and quiet. He was a lovely Christian. He ordered the people to render him divine honors. He kept in his palace 300 young girls and the same number of boys, to minister to his burning passions. He condemned to death his most faithful ministers, senators and servants. His wife and sister fell victims to his cruel malignity; and at last he died an ignominious death at the hands of Mircia, a favorite concubine.

Zephyrinus, who commenced his career as Pope in 203, banished the wise Tertulian and his coadjutors. Origen flourished at this time ; was recalled by this Pope from banishment, and restored to popular favor. He carried his opposition to the freelovers to such an extent, as to become a eunuch. He taught a great many absurd things, and among them some exalted truths: such as "the materiality of mind, final annihilation of evil, and eternal progress." In almost every respect, except his self-mutilation, he was a spiritualist, and as such, opposed the freelove practices of his cotemporaries. During the see of Cornelus, who began his papal career in 252, there were several schisms in the Church, and with them other noteworthy developments; the Ante-pope Norictian, was elected Bishop, in the midst of a debauch. Another freeloving Christian, Fellicissimus corrupted the holy virgins, and was guilty of various other crimes. A young Christian of Alexandria, the heir of a rich patrimony, fell in love with his sister; after being detected in the incest by his brother-in-law, he became frightened, had a vision, and was promised pardon by an angel, on condition that he would live a life of solitude; this was the origin of the celebrated religious order called Anchorites, and this, the first one of all. Thus commenced one pious society.

In the time of Lucius, 2531, it was customary for young virgins to lay with the priests, monks, etc. etc., and thereby mortify the flesh. St. Cyprian justified this practice.

The reign of Denis, the next Pope, was distinguished by nothing remarkable, except the so-called heresies of Paul and Platinus. Those men were spiritualists; the latter, like the immortal Socrates, affirmed that he had a familiar or attendant spirit. We should not mention these and similar personages, in connection with this subject, did we not always find them opposed, not only to the dogmas of the Church, but to the freelove practices of Priests, Bishops, Monks, etc. Wherever we find a true spiritualist, we find an opposer of immorality of every kind, and deception.

All through, the third century history is but one dark record of crime and immorality, perpetrated, not only with the sanction of the Church itself, but many of its highest dignitaries were the blackest hearted villains. About the beginning of the 4th century, there was a vacancy in the Holy See; at this time the Bishops of Numidia assembled, and elected to that See a Bishop noted for his debaucheries and incests; and according to the legends, after he, (Boniface) was beheaded, they, his followers, in seeking to know the whereabouts of his body, inquired for him as a "thick set man of light complexion, who wears a scarlet mantle, and is a roue and debauchee." We next come to the Imperial rule of Constantine the Great, the father of modern Christianity; and it may truly be dated from his time. He ascended the throne through hypocrisy; and tho' his reign was far preferable to that of the infamous Maxentius, so noted for his debaucheries, (whom he deposed); still he was very far from being a good man. The Common Council of Auvergne took place in his reign; where it was decided priests should not marry. Also the Counsil of Neocessarea, where the Bishops opposed the marriage of Priests because they could draw from them a large revenue by permitting concubinage. The heresies of Arius, assisted by Eusebius, led Constantine to call the celebrated Council of Nice, to decide what should be Bible and what not; and several other matters of minor importance. Then again came up the vexed question of the marriage of Priests, and more strenuous anathemas against it; seeming to prefer any amount of crime and beastiality, to the ties of matrimony. St. Athanatius the Great was accused of murder and other heinous crimes; in short, almost all the great Saints and Prelates of that day, were guilty of some great crime. He was finally banished by Tiberius. The reign of Pope Damosas is a history of freeloveism from beginning to end; he was, if possible, more sensual than his predecessors. He was found guilty of repeated adulteries. The Priests, his follwers, bore similar characters, even speculated out of their debaucheries. Under his papal rule, there was a sect called Precillianists, who condemned marriage, and held their meetinings in a state of nudity. So, it seems naked circles were held in those days, by a sect of professed Christians. Well, they were only following in a little different form, the example of the Prophet Isaiah, as related in (Is. 20.) But when Christians accuse us moderns of such practices, without any proof, except bare assertions, we choose to point them continually to the historical proof of the looseness of their ancestors. The whole of the fourth century, like those that preceded, was a bloody page, wherein King and Pope seemed to vie with each other in deeds of violence. Nor was the fifth any better in this respect. Anastatius combined with a courtezan to condemn the Reformer Rutinus, in the year 406. Vigilent, another reformer, spoke boldly against the corruption of the Church, but like his predecessors failed to accomplish any change for the better. Sixtus the third, another of the Popes, was guilty of violating a sacred virgin, and also of incest; and Leo first, noted for his cruel torture of the aged Pricillian; and many other pious rascals flourished in that age. Hormsidas signalized himself by his excessive ambition, and implacable fanaticism—persecuting, scourging and sending into exile, both men and women. Boniface second was guilty of simony, together with Dioscorus and others, the violent and passionate Virgillius, who, in a burst of rage killed a young child, who refused his infamous caresses; whose life was a long train of excesses, crime and perfidy of every description, was at last made a Saint. Says one historian : " his history is one catalogue of horrors, and abominations." Saint Gregory first poisoned a Bishop, discovered Purgatory, whether in consequence of his own misdeeds is not told, and wrote letters of praise to that execrable Queen Brunahaut, because she gave large sums of money to appease divine wrath. Yet he was one of the most zealous persecutors of all heretics, magicians, wizzards, *and those that had familiar spirits,* attributing their power to the Devil, like some modern Priests. He commanded all subordinates to give up their concubines, which was the cause of infanticide to such an extent, that six thousand heads of new-born infants were at one time found in one of the Pope's artificial ponds, on drawing it off to make some repairs. This is corroborated by several historians, prominent among whom is DeCormenin, in his history of the Popes, to which we are indebted for much useful information and assistance in compiling this work. The seventh century was noted for a number of villainous fellows, prominent among whom was Pope Sergius First, who spoiled the Church to get rid of rivals, and made new ordinances against the marriage of priests —he forbid the priests of Africa from keeping their concubines in the interior of their palaces. The populace of that time were so bad that it was necessary to forbid priests solemnizing incestuous marriages. He was accused of incontinence, adultery and other crimes; once, when a young boy was brought him as his son, he got out of it by baptising him, and making the child say, "Sergius not my father." Most of the leading men of the Church at that time, were guilty of now almost unheardof barbarities.

The eighth century began with Constantine First as Pope, who cruelly caused Felix to be besieged in his metropolis, and then caused his tongue to be torn out, and his eyes burned out with a red hot iron —as he also served the Patriarch Callinicus. Pope Stephen Sixth was another of the same stripe. The people became so bad in the time of Adrian First, that Charlemagne, Emperor of the French, when he visited Rome, complained of the dissoluteness of the Priests —he branded them with the most aprobrious epithets; "accused them of dealing in slaves, selling young girls to the Saracens, keeping gambling houses and brothels, and scandalizing Christianity generally." Adrian tried to excuse them by laying their crimes upon others, but the keen intellect of the French Emperor could see through the subterfuges of the Pope, though he was himself a Catholic. Even the Bishops kept concubines. When accused of it they shut up their concubines and eunuchs in their Episcopal residences. They finally became so bad that an ecclesiastical council was called, and Adrian was obliged to condemn them, however much against his will, or do worse —incur the wrath of Charlemagne.

Leo Third was too good a man for the Church, for, says history, "their principal virtues were hypocrisy, avarice and luxury," so they conspired against him, but were foiled in their plans. This brings us to the sixth century, and still we trace this freelove idea; not a moment is it lost sight of in the life and practice of the highest Church Dignitaries. Aye, more, the freelovers we have yet found, are among Popes, Bishops, Priests and Prelates; those whom the world has looked upon as the vicegerents of God on earth. From the traditional account of the giving up of the Keys of Heaven to St. Peter, up to this, the sixth century, the Church still increased in power and wickedness; stronger and still stronger grew the chains in their hold upon the consciences of the people; greater and more iniquitous grew the crimes of the Popes and Clergy. Yet man, outside of the Church was advancing in science, philosophy and everything else. Yet the

Church, with all its power, seemed to be exercised then as now, for the subjugation of human reason; still, we trace it further in our next chapter, from the sixth to the fourteenth century, and as it gains in strength, we find Emperors courting favor of the Popes, instead of Popes obedient to Emperors; and ever the truth of our assertion is seen, that the subjugation of human reason to faith, belief and opinion, is the greatest stumbling block in the way of rapid progress; and when reason is thus trampled under foot, vice and immorality are the legitimate results.

CHAPTER IV.

CONTINUATION OF CATHOLIC HISTORY, FROM THE SIXTH TO THE FOURTEENTH CENTURY; DEBAUCHERY OF POPES AND PRIESTS. OPINIONS OF VARIOUS HISTORIANS, &c.

In the seventh and eighth centuries, the Popes grew more cruel and arbitrary in their rule; binding the yoke of oppression still firmer upon the necks of the people, who, in their debaucheries and crime, but imitated their ecclesiastical leaders. Pascal First, like some of his predecessors, caused his rebellious subjects to loose their eyes and tongues, and added perjury to his long list of crimes. Sergius Second allowed the Priests every license; he sanctioned the abduction and rape of the beautiful Emengarde, daughter of Lothaire, by a vassal of King Charles. The knavery of the Priests is spoken of by all historians as one of the prominent items of that time. Leo Second founded a convent of nuns in his own house, and abandoned himself with them to all manner of looseness. These charges are sustained by the admissions of a multitude of worthy historians.

In 853 a very remarkable occurrence took place; no less an event than the reign of a female Pope, or Popess Joan. This wonderful person, the only woman that ever donned the Papal robe, was an illegitimate child; when she grew to womanhood she was very beautiful, and loved, and was beloved in turn by a young monk. She donned male attire, and with her companion traveled over most of the countries of Europe. She distinguished herself for her learning and piety—confounding the wisdom of the Grecian and Roman Sages—all this while disguised as a monk, wandering with her paramour, who finally died, leaving her desolate in a strange land. She continued her studies, however, and increased in religious lore and tactics, till finally, by intrigue, she gained the fullness of her hopes, the Papal Chair. She was a good ruler, but could not long control her strong passions. At last she took a young priest for a lover, by whom she became enciente. Then, as goes the legend, an angel appeared to her and told her she could have her choice, to be either delivered up to Satan forever, or be exposed as a woman, to all Rome. She chose the latter, and expired in the streets of Rome, in the midst of a large procession in the pains of childbirth. What an awful picture! Nicolas First, was her successor. His reign was replete with dissensions. The celebrated Photius wrote him a scathing letter, in which he rebuked the Latin Church, as tending to encourage adulterous, incestuous, ravishers, homicides, etc.," which crimes were very common at that time. Adrian Second, it seems had a wife and daughter; a Bishop's son seduced the daughter, and finally murdered both her and her mother. John Eighth, died a violent death from poison administered to him by the relatives of a Roman lady, whose husband he had carried off to minister to his unnatural passions. The Catholic historian, Baronius, called the ninth century "the age of ignorance." Yet the Church had great and continually increasing power. Never, said he, "did Priests, and especially Popes, commit so many adulteries, rapes, incests, robberies, murders and unbridled debaucheries. The palace of the Popes became a disgraceful tavern, in which ecclesiastics of all nations disputed with harlots the price of infamy. Nor was the next century, the tenth, any better, for in the time of Benedict Fourth, says the learned Platinius, "the Priests abandoned the regularity of their lives, and went to sleep in the arms of corruption." The chains of humility and chastity, became the end of all ambition; the recompense of all crime." Edgar, King of England, in a speech to the Bishops of his Kingdom, said: "The See of Rome is but the head of debauchery, drunkenness and impurity. The houses of Priests have become the shameful retreats of prostitutes, jugglers and Sodomites. They gamble by night and day in the house of the Pope; bachanalian songs and lascivious dances, have taken the place of fasting and prayer." Glabert Budolphe who assisted in the revelries of this period, says: "All were abandoned without shame to the joys of luxury and pleasure, and expended in their origies with courtezans the money of the poor." Sergius third was noted for his amours with the infamous Marozia. John the Tenth, the next Pope, was very handsome. Theodora, the mistress of a former Pope became enamored of him; he yielded to the passion, and thereby paved the way to the Papal Chair; he afterwards joined with the notorious Marozia in sacriligious commerce. She finally became jealous and caused his death. John Eleventh, her son, became Pope in 931. This abominable woman, then in all the splendor of her fatal beauty, wished to make sure of her rule over the mind of the young Pope; by becoming his mistress she did so, and abandoned herself with him, to incestuous intercourse with her own son. Then was seen on the Chair of St. Peter, a man who left the shameless arms of his mother, to appear in the holiest ceremonies of religion; and Priests on their knees before a woman, who surpassed in her lusts the most shameless courtezan of Rome. This Pope also died an ignominious death in captivity. Young Octavian, son of the Patrician Alberic, himself the son and lover of Marozia, then became Pope, as **John Twelfth, in 956.** He was of tender age, yet his infamous mother initiated him into all the mysteries of the most shameful debaucheries. Theophilactus ruled over the corrupted clergy of the Greek Church, commencing a patriarch of sixteen, he ruled, at the same time he gave himself up to the most criminal, and disgraceful actions; made no consecrations except for money, which he spent upon courtezans, etc. The whole life of **Pope John Twelfth, is** a freelove record of the most revolting character. He was deposed at one time; then reinstated; was surprised in adultery, and slain by an incensed husband in the very arms of his mistress.

Pope Boniface Seventh sold the sacred ornaments and crucifixes to support his mistresses. He was deposed, and again re-instated by murder and knavery; was finally killed, and his dead body dragged through the streets of Rome. Pope John Ffteenth was accused of pillaging the Church, and ravaging the temples and religious houses, to enrich his mistresses and minions. And Gregory Fifth, re-instated, closed the century.

Pope Sylvester Second, ushered in the next. Historians disagree as to his character. Catholics decry him because of his sorsery, or mediumship, but as far as we can learn, he was superior in point of morals to most of his predecessors and cotemporaries. The eleventh century was also remarkable for a mixture of gross superstition and horrid debauchery. Benedict Eighth complained of the licentiousness of the Priests, called all their children bastards, and railed severely about a married priesthood. He disgraced the Church by his debaucheries and extortions. The subtle Monk, Hildebrand, commenced his career and intriguing for Priestly and Papal power about this time, 1040. Leo Ninth, then Pope, tried to reform the clergy and the people; he consequently had a great many intricate and dificult cases to decide. One Gregory, Bishop of Verciel, was up on a charge of adultery with a young widow. The Prelate went immediately to the Sovereign of the Church, and offered a large sum of money, for which he was not only absolved, but permitted still to continue the connection. Peter Damian also addressed a letter to Leo, asking advice. "We have," wrote he, "Prelates who openly abandon themselves to all kinds of debauchery, get drunk at their feasts, and keep their concubines in Episcopal Palaces." He also cites some of the remarkable rules of punishment adopted by these Prelates. "A Priest who is not a Monk, who *sins accidental*, with a virgin, shall perform two years penance, i. e., fast on bread and water four days of three lents; or if the virgin be consecrated to God, five years; a Clerk for the same fault, six months, etc." Leo replied to him that he wished reform, but that the number of criminals was so great, he was obliged to tolerate their crimes. So his plan for reforming the clergy was a total failure. Alexander Second, in 1066, condemned marriages of relatives; which was the cause of the formation of an order called the Society of the Incestuous, who sanctioned such unions: they did not however, oppose the prevailing religion. He afterwards declared that simony was no crime, and if he deposed simoniacal and adulterous priests, it was only to get pay for their absolution. At length, the ambitious Hildebrand, the poisoner of Popes, after having buried eight Pontiffs, who were in their turn the instruments of his ambition, mounted the Papal Chair in 1073. Himself the fruit of an incestuous amour, while a Monk, he at first made great pretence and show of morality, but being surprised in adultery with a servant girl, he relaxed his rigor, and authorized the Monks to keep women in their Convents. He anathematized marriage, was a practical freelover, and forbade married Priests assisting at divine service. The French Clergy opposed this decision, and sent him a scathing letter, from which we take the following quotations: "You are a heretic, Most Holy Father, since you teach such an insensate morality. As for you, Oh, Sacriligious Pontiff! whose debaucheries with young Monks, and adulteries with the Countess Matilda, and her mother, are public scandal. We learn that you would lead Priests into your disorders, causing them to separate from their wives." And this Hildebrand, was the man that did more to establish the Church in temporal as well as spiritual power, than any who lived before him. The first crusades were instituted under the patronage of Urban Second. Peter the Hermit preached the first sermon 1085. While these holy wars were going on through the reign of Urban and Pascal Second, the Church itself was in a very depraved condition, Says Bernard DeMorlaix, Monk of Clerny : " Pure souls exist no longer; fraud, impurity, and crime of every description, such as rapine, wars, quarrels, incests and murders desolate the Church; Rome is the impure city of the hunter Nimrod, piety and religion have deserted her walls. The Pontiff, or rather the King of this Babylon, (Pascal) tramples under foot the gospel, and causes himself to be adored as God." Honorious, Priest of Antrim says : " Behold these Bishops and Cardinals of Rome! these unworthy ministers who surround the Throne of the Beast; they are constantly occupied with new iniquities, and never cease committing crime; not only do these wretches abandon themselves to all kinds of depravity, with young deacons, but they even wish to oblige the Clergy of all the Provinces to imitate them. Thus in all the Churches, they neglect the divine service, soil the priesthood by their impurities. Look also at these Monks; knavery, and hypocrisy shelter themselves beneath their cowls, Their holy frocks cover cupidity and Sodomy. Examine these convents of nuns —the Beast has made his bed in their dormitories; their couches are defiled by the most horrid debaucheries; these abominable girls no longer choose the Virgin for their model, but Phryna and Massalina. They do not prostrate themselves before Christ, but before an idol of Priapus."

One of the noted characters who lived during the papal reign of Calixtus Second, was Peter Abelard, one of the most celebrated dialecticians of that century; notorious also for his freelove connection with Heloise. niece of the Canon Fulbert. He was much run after by the women of that day, but his dearest love was Heloise. Her father discovering their amours, wished them married; but she would not consent, saying, " let me be mistress to the man I love." (This has been celebrated by Pope the Poet, in his ballad called Heloise and Abelard.) It is said by some writers that they finally consented to a private marriage.

The second crusade commenced in the time of Eugenius Third, 1145. In the midst of that Church were all the holy wars concocted. Of the thirteenth century a Monk of St. Albans, named Mathew Paris, says: "The Holy City has become a prostitute, whose shameless debaucheries, surpass those of Sodom and Gomoroah." St. Francis, the founder of the order of Franciscans, lived at this period. He performed a great many silly actions, was a notorious Sodomite, and even went so far as to call his unnatural connections with one Marcus, "sacred love." Nicolas Fifth first instituted Inquisitions, and desecrated the dead bodies of his enemies. Menard, Count Tyrol, says of the Clergy of his reign: "Give to the Bishops your robe, and they will want your mantle; who can be so stupid, so cowardly, as to endure without complaining, the cupidity, avarice and debauchery of these wretches? The occupation of the Priests is to get bastards, preside over orgies, and extort money from the people. We have been long enough under their feet, let us rise and exclaim, death to these enemies of humanity!"

Pope Boniface Eighth caused the unfortunate Celestin to be placed in a dungeon, and starved to death. He was so cruel that he was given over by the Priests as sure to be damned. John Villani calls him "a cruel, ambitious, corrupt Priest." This Pope gave the following freelove maxim, among others of a similar character: "It is no greater sin to abandon oneself to carnal pleasure with a young boy, or girl, than to rub ones hands together."

At the dawn of the fourteenth century, we find the Church still increased in power and villainy. Robert Gallus, in his symbolic style thus speaks of the Church of that age: "I was in prayer, with my looks toward heaven, when suddenly I perceived a monster clothed in the Pontifical Cape; it had feet in form of a sword, and immense hands, which it plunged into the east and into the west, to draw them out full of gold and precious stones. It having approached me, I heard an infernal voice saying, 'It is the Roman Church.'"

The Cardinals in particular, were noted for their immorality—when they first assembled to elect Clement Fifth, got into a quarrel, broke up, and returned to their Palaces, to resume their habits of debauchery, with their mistresses and minions. He was finally chosen Pope by Philip Archbishop of Bordeaux; who after having his treasury pillaged, to divert his chagrin, retired to Montil with the Countess de Foix, and his minions; they there passed scenes of debauchery so depraved, that it is impossible to relate them; but Clement, already old, was attacked with a bad disease, which finally ended his earthly career. After his death, his treasury was seized and divided among his concubines and hirelings.

Benedict Twelfth, was noted for his attempt to seduce the beautiful sister of the Poet Petrarch, who informed her brother of his advances. He went to the Pope to complain; when this dissolute old Pontiff offered to pay him a large sum of money and a Cardinals Office, for the virginity of his sister. The indignant Poet rejected the infamous proposal, with a virtuous energy. The Pope, out of pure revenge, on account of such refusal, anathematized him, and denounced him as a heretic to the Inquisition. He escaped from Avignon, but was compelled to leave his sister in the care of their brother Gerard. This wretch could not resist the thirst for gold; and in the night, this poor young girl, scarcely sixteen years of age, was carried to the Papal Palace, and given up to the corrupt embraces of this dissolute old man.

During the reign of Pope Clement Sixth, Joan of Naples murdered her husband; from which crime this Pope absolved her, on condition of her becoming his mistress, and delivering into his possession the Kingdom of Avignon. She complied with his wishes. According to various historians, the Court of Avignon, under this Pontificiate, was the receptacle of every vice, and of the most horrible depravity. The Poet Petrarch, has, in his fervent, poetic style, left us the following flowing description of the corruption and crime of the Church:

"Who would not by turns smile with pity, or feel indignation, in seeing these decrepid Cardinals and Prelates, with white hairs, and their ample togas, beneath which lie concealed an impudence and lasciviousness which nothing equals. These libidinous dotards are so forgetful of age and Priesthood, as to fear neither dishonor nor approbrium. They consume their best days in every kind of excess and libertinage. These unworthy Priests think to arrest time, which drags them along, and believe themselves young in their old age, because their shamelessness and intemperance, lead them on to saturnalia, repugnant to youth. Thus Satan himself, with infernal laugh, presides over their debauches, places himself between the virgin object of their nauseous amours, and these old dotards, who become astonished to find their strength less than their inclinations. I will say nothing of the adulteries, rapes and incests; these are but the preludes, the beginning of their debauchery. I cannot count the number of women carried off, nor the number of girls violated. I will not speak of the means employed to force outraged husbands, fathers and brothers to silence. I will not tell by what threats, they have been compelled to take back their prostituted wives, children and sisters, bearing in their bosoms the fruit of their amours with these Princes of the Church! outrages which are renewed as soon as the victims are delivered! outrages which cease only when these old men are satiated, tired, disgusted with those whom they have ruined. The people know these things as well as I do, and loudly condemn them; for grief now will I be heard; and threats will no longer awe indignation into silence!"

Petrarch lived at that time, he knew and felt the corruption of the popes and priests, his testimony then is valuable in showing up the depraved condition of the Church in the fourteenth century. With this we close our fourth chapter; a chapter of dark, and gloomy history. Its horrid character consists not in itself, or the charges we bring against the Christian Church, but in the fact of the truth of these charges, and their relevency to our considered subject. The ponderous machinery of the Catholic Church, was, in all its numerous parts, in full working order at this time. There were, as yet, no Protestants to take from their power, or divide with them the spoils. Kings and princes did the Church homage, and kneeled to receive the blessings of the pope. To him, and his assistant priests, the world looked for absolution from the consequences of sin.

CHAPTER V.

CONCLUSION OF CATHOLIC HISTORY, FROM THE 14TH CENTURY TO THE PRESENT TIME. *PRACTICAL FREELOVEISM OF THE POPES, CARDINALS, ETC.; THEIR HORRID CRUELTIES AND PERSECUTIONS IN THE NAME OF RELIGION.*

Innocent Sixth, when he became Pope, exerted himself to put an end to a great number of abuses, that had become customs at the Court of Rome; especially the rights which the officers of the apostolic confederacy granted in the name of the Church, to tolerate prostitutes. Officers! yes, high dignitaries of the Holy Church had to be restrained, so great had their licentiousness become. This pope was as austere in his morals, as his predecessor had been corrupt. His reforms were met with ill favor by his Christian subjects. So great had been the license given them under former rulers, it no doubt seemed hard to have all their special privileges taken away. In the latter part his life, Innocent changed his tactics, turned suddenly to a wild fanatic, and persecuted all heretics with the utmost rigor.

This severity was shown most particularly against the Fratricelli, a class of people who dared to speak the truth, in regard to the infamous character of former popes. John of Chattillon, one of these unfortunate men, cried out while burning at the stake, as follows:— "Christians, my brethren, I declare before God, who judges us, you are the dupes of the knavery of the Pope. In the name of my salvation, I affirm that John 22d, Benedict 12th, Clement 6th, and Innocent 6th are swindlers, forgers, robbers, murderers and heretics."

Charles 4th, having learned that the Pope had re-established his high authority, came to him in the most abject humility, as he had before to other pontiffs; no prince had shown so much subserviency to the Pope, as he. The poet Petrarch addressed him a stinging letter, which closed with the following plain language—speaking of the Pope, to whom Charles had acknowledged obedience:

"It is gold alone which can appease this monster; enchain him with gold, and you may ravish your sisters or murder your father; with gold you can open heaven, buy the saints, angels, the virgin, the holy spirit, Jesus Christ, and the Eternal Father himself. The pope will sell anything for gold, except his tiara."

Like the voice of an avenging angel, came the words of the poet to the mind of the recreant prince, and he soon after saw the justice of this scathing rebuke. Others, also, arose and condemned the usurpationss of the pope, which continued until his death, at an advanced age—generally condemned for his cruelty, as he had before been loved for his morality.

In the time of Gregory 11th, there appeared a young nun, Saint Catherine, who claimed wonderful revelations; even went so far as to claim that she was married to Christ. She had a secret interview with the pope, who was wonderfully pleased with her, so much so that he gave her full power to make a treaty with a rebellious nation, (the Florentines,) on her own terms. What if some ambitious young woman now, should say she was married to Christ, or even assert she was wedded to a disembodied spirit, or even controlled by a spirit to give important revelations about affairs of government? What a hue and cry would be raised; the Devil would be called on as her attend-

and guide, or insanity be called her only spouse. But this silly girl was made a Saint, and as such is still in the holy catalogue of the Church of Rome. The times then and now are slightly different. About this time (1378), in the reign of Urban 6th, the great western schism took place, and Clement 7th was made Pope at Avignon, while Urban reigned at Rome. It is difficult to tell which of these two popes was the best capable ruling; the dissolute Urban, or Clement, whose vices are thus enumerated by the historian, Father Maimburg:

"Among his principal vices, luxuriousness held the first place. He chose from preference, his mistresses from his own family, and loaded them with riches, honors and dignities."

Urban induced Charles de Duras to assassinate his foster mother, Joanna, in the most cruel and indecent manner. He also put all his conquered enemies to death, with frightful torture, and finally died of poison at the hands of the agents of Clement. This excited but little regret. The latter died about five years after. Dr. Clenngis has pronounced the following judgment upon this pope:

"There never existed a more miserable priest, a more cowardly and servile flatterer. He gave Bishoprics and Abbeys to the minions of princes, and it finally happened that the mere buffoons of the Duke of Bery were as much pope as Clement."

The fifteenth century finds the Church still reeking with physical and spiritual degradation. Says history, the Churches became the resorts of robbers, sodomites, and assassins. Popes, Cardinals and Bishops exercised robbery forcibly in the provinces, and employed, as was most convenient, poison, the sword, and fire, to free themselves from their enemies, and despoil their victims. The Inquisition was also in full force, and lent its horrible ministry to popes and Kings. The country was covered with legions of priests and monks, who devoured the substance of the people, and carried off to their impure retreats, young girls and boys, whom they again cast out, disgraced and dishonored. The cities became the theatres of orgies and saturnalia, and the palaces of Bishops filled with troops of courtezans, minions, jugglers and buffoons. To all these causes of demoralization was joined the great schism, which divided Europe, and caused torrents of blood to flow. Gregory 12th professed great mildness of character, even went so far as to offer to abdicate in order to settle the difficulties which divided the Church. But he afterward clothed himself with great dignity, and declared he had made no promise which he was bound to fulfill. He assumed the most arrogant authority over all Cardinals and priests; which so incensed a number of the principal men, that they escaped from his power and went to Pisa. They then published a manifesto against Gregory, stating as a good reason for leaving, that he wished to murder several of them. The pope anathematized them as heretics, and forbade all the faithful from communing with them. They in turn cursed the pope, and according to Theodore de Niem, wound up their article with the following facts:

"You, Gregory, we will unveil all your turpitudes, and your incestuous amours with your own sister. We will cite you before *our* tribunal at Pisa, and depose you from the Holy See."

Finally, both popes, Benedict and Gregory, were cited before this tribunal. Neither appeared. The venerable patriarch of Alexandria then mounted the pulpit, and pronounced as follows:

"In the name of Jesus Christ, we declare that these two infamous men are guilty of enormous iniquities and excesses, that they should be cut off from the Church, and rejected by God; consequently they are as such deposed."

Alexander 5th, was, according to Theodore de Niems, unfortunate in allowing his scandalous beastiality to be publicly known; he was intoxicated regularly every night; was finally poisoned by a favorite Cardinal, named Balthasa Cosa, who succeeded him as John 23d. He was in early life a pirate, but afterwards turned priest, in the reign of Boniface 9th. In a short time, by various extortions, he became very wealthy, and committed all manner of crimes with impunity. He introduced himself secretly into the cells of nuns, for the vilest purposes, and carried on an incestuous amour with his brother's wife. Indeed, he became so open in his debaucheries, that Boniface, shameless wretch as he was, was forced to send him away from his Court. He sent him on a mission to subdue the people of Bologna. He there found himself absolute master, and gave himself up to his unbridled passions, there were no boys or girls of any rank who could believe themselves secure from the power of this infamous priest. Parents who dared to dispute the right of this monster, were plunged into the dungeons of the Inquisition. And as it were by refinement of lubricity, he abused the children in the very presence of their parents and friends, while they were put to the torture. Gregory anathematized him, and at last he became pope, as we have stated by committing murder. He celebrated his triumph by the most disgusting orgies, and seemed to strive to outdo all former tyrants in ferocity, cruelty and licentiousness. He resorted to all manner of cruelty to extort money from the people. On one occasion he invited all the Cardinals and wealthiest Church Dignitaries to a magnificent feast, and after they had become drunk with wine, levied contributions upon them. Those who declined assisting at these orgies, none the less escaped his cupidity. He would put them to the torture to make them "untie their purse," as he expressed it. All the wealth he thus wrested from the people was divided among his concubines and minions. Yet this pope was very bitter against all heretics; excommunicated Wickliffe, and condemned all his books to be burned wherever found; and among the numerous classes sentenced to be given over to the Inquisition without reserve, " were all those who used magic, divination or enchantment; and all those who made agreements with spirits, to obtain power from them." So, this old freelovor was not a Spiritualist, but a most orthodox persecutor of everything of the kind; fearing, no doubt, that his own dark plots would be revealed, if the mediums, then called majicians and sorcerers, were permitted to live. The King of Naples at last became incensed against him, and tracked him like a wild beast, from one place to another, as he sought to evade being brought before the King. The Cardinals who accompanied him were seized with a panic, and fled. John alone waited for his enemy unalarmed. The reason was simple—he had taken measures to have him poisoned by one of his mistresses. Monstrelot, a cotemporary chronicler, thus speaks of the death of the King·

" He could not live long, because he was too much abandoned to debauchery, and created too much hatred by his cruelties; poison only hastened his decline."

Thus he died, poisoned in an infamous manner; and one of his mistresses, bribed by John XXIII, became the instrument of the Pope's vengeance. This Pope was finally deposed—his whole papal career was reeking with all manner of crimes of the darkest dye—he was succeeded by Martin V, who was a great diplomatist and a very great rascal. His disputes with the Spaniards drew against him a formidable array; several Cardinals even wished to depose him. A satire, called the "Mass of Simony," appeared about this time—a very curious and cutting piece of sarcasm. This was handed to the Pope, who determined to leave the place where he then was, (Constance) at once. His train on this occasion, says Reichaubal, "surpassed im magnificence all that had been before seen. Martin rode with his tiara on his head, and the housings of his horse were of purple and gold; behind the Pope came his parasol bearer, and marched in squadrons, on foot and on horseback, nobles, soldiers, priests, monks, all the trades, and the seven hundred and eighteen courtezans of the Holy Council, dressed in white and marching two by two." (Exceeding by eighteen the number of Solomon's wives). This Pope caused the death of John, his predecessor, by poison, and died himself of apoplexy 1431. He was a tyranical ruler, loved pomp, show and grandeur; never lost a single occasion to augment the power of the Church, which was to him valuable only as a means of personal aggrandizement.

Eugenius IV, succeeded him. He was a cruel wretch, noted particularly for his cruelties to Masius, which so exasperated the people, that for a time his life was in imminent danger. He was finally deposed.

In 1455 commenced the reign of that terrible family of Borgias; whose names have the world over been as synonymous with every species of villany Alphonso Borgia ascended the Papal Chair un the title of Calixtus III. He lived but a short time, and left his immense wealth to his infamous nephews, Peter and Roderick, who afterward used it to purchase the tiara. All the Popes of this age seem to have been unusually cruel. Paul III condemned to torture the celebrated historian Platinus, in a manner too horribly indecent to describe. He said "learning was useless, and all science opposed to religion." How much that sounds like modern priests, who decry reason, and all new religious discoveries as opposed to the true religion, viz: their opinions; many of whom lack only the power to make them second Pope Pauls; like him, ever ready to despise that of which they are themselves ignorant, as of no value to others, and a curse to the world at large. No doubt there are many now, who would like to impale the present historian for giving the people facts with regard to the characters of these men, who assume to be God's vicegerents on earth. But the power is lacking, for we live in a free and enlightened republic.

Of Sixtus IV, it is affirmed by Onuphre Machiavel and Peter Valateran, "that the Holy Father conducted himself outrageously when a Cardinal. He was engaged in amous with each of his sisters, and went so far as to use his monstreus debaucheries to young children, the fruits of his own amours with his eldest sister. Never had the cities of Sodom and Gomoroah been the theatre of such abominations." Besides, one of the first acts of Sixtus, was to publish a bull in which he declared "that the nephews and bastards of Popes, should be of right Roman princes." He showed himself to be a tyranical monster, abusive to his superiors in intelligence, frowning upon everything of a progressive nature, giving his patronage to the low and vile, and showed himself the ardent protector of the courtezans of Rome. Cornelius Agrippa relates very gravely, and sanctimoniously the fact, "that his Holiness founded several noble lupanars, in which each girl was taxed a golden Julius a week. This impost brought in more than twenty thousand ducats a year. Prostitutes were placed in these resorts of depravity, by the Prelates of the Apostolic Court, who levied a certain tax upon their products." This infamous pontiff also permitted Peter, a Cardinal and patriarch of Constantinope, Jerome his brother, and the Cardinal of St. Lucia, to exercise horrible iniquities during the months of June, July and August, and with his own hand wrote at the bottom of the request, "Be it as desired."

Innocent VIII had sixteen bastards when he ascended the Papal Chair, and like his predecessors, took good care to get them good places in the various principalities. Stephen Infesura also maintains " that this **Holy Father**, in his last sickness, attempted to re-animate the sources of life by means of a frightful beverage, composed by a **Jewish** physician, of the blood of three young boys, slain for the purpose." Onuphre and Ciaconius maintain the same facts, which they place at a much earlier **period**.

We have now reached the culminating point of Roman iniquity. As we draw to the close of the fifteenth century, we begin to see the light of civilization and philosophy peering up in the distance, and and taking stronger hold of the minds of the masses; and though Popes, Cardinals and prelates, **seem to vie** with their predecessors **and** each other in vice and crime, as the people **become** enlightened, they begin, slowly at first, to throw off the galling chains of spiritual and temporal bondage. It is also seen, that as these self-styled ministers of God have lost sight of the spirit world, and attendant angels, they have more and more merged into temporal rule. And as the desire for spiritual knowledge leaves the mind of man, or his spiritual friends are taken far away from him by false theology, he must have knowledge, he must have pleasure: and so he turns to the low, the licentious and criminal, or strives for personal aggrandizement **and power**. This we see particularly manifest in the character of the **Borgias, Leo X, Julien II, Pius VI, and others** of like form of mental organism. The accession and reign of **the** notorious Roderick Borgia is called by historians, the period **when** the theocracy had attained the apogee of its glory, in which, far from concealing its corruptions in the dark, it exposes them to the light of day, even glories in them. This being, [Borgia] was one of the greatest villains **and** debauchees that ever lived. The very record of his crimes **is enough to** make a stout heart quake with fear. His freelove adventures alone, would fill volumes. We will relate a few of the best athenticated

He formed a liason with a Spanish lady and her two daughters; after having seduced the mother, he corrupted her children, and initiated them into his horrid pleasures. He afterwards freed himself from the eldest, and kept near him the youngest and handsomest, the notorious Rosa Vanozza, who was by him the mother of Francis, Cæsar, Godfrey, and also the celebrated Lucretia Borgia, so well known in connection with the most shameless debaucheries, wrought into plays and operas, even down to the present time.

In the reign of his uncle Calixtus, Roderick was called to Rome, where he had many high offices bestowed on him; he then professed great morality, and affected the life of an Anchorite. He never appeared in public except with his hands crossed on his breast, and his eyes bent to the ground. While he was thus playing on the credulity of the gullible public at Rome, he still carried on a correspondence with Rosa. In the following extract from one of his letters to her, which history has preserved, he gives the reason for the farce he is playing.

"Rosa, my well beloved, imitate my example, remain chaste until it shall become in my power to reach thee, and mingle our love in infinite pleasures; let no other mouth profane thy charms, no other hand lift those veils which conceal my sovereign good. A little more patience and he who is called my uncle, will bequeath me the chair of St. Peter, as a heritage. In the meantime take great pains in the education of our children, for they are destined to govern people and Kings."

He was disappointed, however, in these hopes; and being no longer able to restrain himself, he returned to his former course of life, as Captain of the Adventurers, and committed so many murders and rapes, that Henry, King of Castile, drove him out of Spain. On his return to Rome, he brought Rosa and his children, whom he passed off as belonging to his Intendent; and every night he abandoned himself with her, and his daughter Lucretia, to the most shameful debaucheries.

Finally, on the death of Innocent, he bought up the votes of a majority of the Cardinals. To most he gave magnificent offices, houses and lands; one vote he bought with the virtue of his daughter,(what little was left,) and was proclaimed Pope, as Alexander VI. "At last," said he, solemnly, "I am Pope, the Vicar of Christ on earth." He then showed himself in his true character, and no longer strove to conceal his monstrous crimes. Paul Langius affirms, "that he turned Rome into a perfect slaughter-house; his ruling passion was an unmeasured ambition for the elevation of his bastards. He gave them each kingdoms of their own. At the first marriage of Lucretia, says Stephen Infesura, "there were lassivious orgies, worthy of that infamous woman;" even after her marriage, says Burchard, Master of Ceremonies to the Pope, "she did not leave the apartments of the Holy Father, by day or night." She also presided over the Council of Cardinals in the costume of Bachante, with naked bosom, and body scarce covered with a muslin robe," Her behavior on these occasions, was so immodest, that Burchard, accustomed as he was to such scenes, exclaims, in recording it, "horror, ignominy and disgrace!" He was a favorite of the Pope, and an eye witness of these scenes, therefore his testimony cannot be gainsayed. Some portions of his records are too vulgar and indecent to be translated.

Cæsar had a falling out with his father, but was afterward reconciled. He and his attendants, to celebrate this last event, spent four whole days, says Thomaso Thomassi, "in the woods of Ostia, taking pleasure in surpassing in debaucheries and licentlousness, all the most depraved imagination could invent. After which they returned to that Rome which they had rendered a cavern of brigands, a sanctuary of iniquity. It would be impossible to relate all the murders, rapes and incests, which were daily committed at the Court of the Pope."

The whole life of this infamous Pope and his family, is one vast record of freeloveism of the most unnatural kind. We will quote one more incident from history, in regard to them, and go on to the consideration of other personages. The third marriage of Lucretia, says Burchard, "was celebrated by saturnalia, which had never yet been equalled, even by this corrupt Court. His Holiness supped with his Cardinals, and the great Dignitaries of the Court, each having by his side two courtezans, who had no other dress but thin muslin robes and a garland of flowers. When the repast was over, they, to the number of fifty, performed lascivious dances, first alone, then with the Cardinals. Finally, at a signal from Lucretia, their robes fell off, mid the applause of the Holy Father." (The remainder of the proceedings will not bear translation.) That was a naked circle with pompous surroundings and high authority; not like the ancient Nicolaites, and Pricillians, who were obliged to be very secret about their gatherings; and from whom, we think, Prof. Felton, and others of like ilk, must have got their ideas of these things, as it has been proved that such things do not exist now, the assertions of these would-be wise men to the contrary notwithstanding.

But the Borgias being God's chosen people on earth, I suppose the good Catholics would say, (or good Protestants either if they belonged to their Church,) that they had a right to do these things, and we freethinkers are very naughty to pry into the hidden mysteries of the Holy Church. But the character of these persons was so openly infamous, that no one can deny the historical facts. Even Catholics, if they are intelligent, and talking to intelligent people, will not attempt to justify the course of Alexander VI, and his minions. This Pope finally died of poison, in the year 1503. A fit end to such a life of infamy and crime.

Julius II, was in early life a pirate, and followed the business of capturing young girls, and selling them to the Turks. At his death a bitter satire appeared, attributed to the learned Erasmus, "in which Julius is represented in a scene with the Prince of Apostles; the latter refuses him entrance to the Kingdom of Heaven, and reproaches him with all his crimes. He accuses him of incest with his sister, and daughter, of vile crimes with his bastards, nephews, and several Cardinals; he calls him a drunkard, robber, murderer and poisoner; and declares to him that the Gates of Heaven are closed to all who died of the disease which he did."

Next in order comes Leo X, an intellectual villain, with just knowledge enough to carry on his nefarious undertakings. Though filled with a loathesome disease, he came to the assembly of Cardinals, (before his election as Pope,) borne on a litter. He was openly an impious man before his election, and made fun of the very office he was most anxious to obtain. As soon as he was installed in the Holy See, he abandoned himself to luxury and debauchery. He banished the brutal debaucheries of the Borgias, and their sattellites, and established a species of gallantry less revolting, though quite as dangerous to morality. Hanelot de la Housage, relates many scandalous adventures of this Pope, in connection with certain ladies of the Court. One, concerning one of the mistresses of Francis, King of France, named Marie Gaudin, who was very beautiful. This attracted the attention of Leo, and by an agreement between him and Francis, she yielded to the possession of the Pope, who gave her as a memento, a jewel of great value."

It was during the Pontificiate of Leo, that Luther appeared, and launched forth his thunders against the Court of Rome, and the iniquities of the Catholic Church. He sounded the trumpet of alarm, after visiting the Holy City, and seeing for himself the wrongs practiced in the name of Christ. The following is a specimen of his language:

"People listen! I come in the name of the Most High, to point out for your execration, the abominable Pontiff who presses you down."

These were the words, and this the man that caused the Pope to tremble in his Chair, led the people to a more thorough investigation into the character of their rulers. He was a sort of medium—his cotemporaries say, "He spoke like one inspired." He ridiculed the idea of a man God, and boldly exposed the simoniacal practices of the Popes and Prelates. He went from place to place, and with his impassioned eloquence gave the light which had been given him from the higher world. The Pope sent an order to Charles V, to have him arrested, to be judged and condemned by the Holy Iniquisition. This was easier said than done. Charles wrote back to the Pope, "that it would not be safe to attempt it, just then." So the Pope was forced to content himself with sending a bull against him, his works, and his followers. Luther burned this in public, and went, voluntarily, to the Diet of Worms, to meet the Popes legates. He also offered to discuss with the Catholics, some seventy propositions. But, no! they were afraid of discussion, (as are the Priests of all denominations at the present day.) The result of all this was the building up of the first sect of Protestants that ever successfully opposed the Church of Rome. Cordolier Thomas, a celebrated preacher of that day, gives the following picture of the morals of the time:

"How long shall we be scandalized by gross adulteries and incests, ye unworthy Priests?" cried he from the gallery of the Cathedral at Bordeaux—" when will you cease to steal money from the poor in order to have a concubine in your bed, and a fat mule in your stable; and all by the grace of the crucifix, and taking the trouble to say Dominis Vobiscum? Curses upon ye, ministers of Satan! who seduce young girls and married females, and who learn from them at confessional, the means of drawing them into sin! Shame on you, Priests of Lucifer! who dare to use the ascendant which your characters give you over credulous minds, in order to initiate the young into carnal pleasures! who make your parsonages houses of infamy, where you keep young girls and boys for lust and infamy! Have I not heard with my own ears, the Curate James boast that he played, swore, drank and fornicated better than any of them?"

Mailard, who had been preacher to Louis XI, thundered with still more force against the disorders of the Priests. Said he:

"I see Abbots, Priests, Monks and Prelates, heaping treasures on treasures, and decoying Christians like pickpockets! I know a Bishop who is served every night at supper, by young girls entirely naked! I know another who keeps a seraglio of young girls, whom he calls prostitutes in moulting! Bishops no longer give away livings but at the request of females; that is to say—when the mother, sisters, nieces or cousins of the candidate, have paid the price of them with their honor! Speak, ye infamous Bishops and Priests! ye blessed simoniacs! ye blessed drunkards and bullies! ye blessed procurers, who gain orders by rendering foul services! Go to the Devil, ye infamous wretches! At the hour of your death, will you dare to present yourselves before Christ, full of wine, and having on your arms the prostitutes you have kept, or your mistress servants, or your nieces, who are most frequently your bastards, and your concubines, or the girls whose dowry you have gained for them by impurity, or the mother from whom you have purchased the virginity of her daughters? Go to all the Devils, cohorts of thieves and pilferers! Come forward, ye female drunkards and robbers, ye priestesses of Venus, who dare say, if a priest gets me with child, I will not be the only one! Come forward nuns, who people the cisterns and ponds of convents with the bodies of new born infants! What frightful accusations would you not hear, if all those children could name their executioners or fathers? My brethren, the time is come, or approaching, in which God will do justice on all this brood of idlers, of mute dogs, of ignorant wretches, of leeches, robbers and murderers!"

No Emperor, King or Pope ever carried his epicureanism so far as Leo X. Thus the highest employments waited the invention of a new ragout. In the festivals of the Vatican, numerous buffoons were employed to enliven the guests by their gay sallies, to which Leo replied, and strove with them in cynicism of Language. Young girls and handsome boys, clothed in oriental costume, and expert in the arts of debauchery had orders to amuse the guests, and these festivities were terminated by orgies only excelled by those of the Borgias. He finally died a miserable death from a fit of anger. The old murderer and lecher, the persecutor of Luther, the glutton and debauchee, perished. What a being to assume control over the consciences of men, to listen to the secrets of the inmost heart, and direct the ponderous machinery of that powerful Church. He belonged to that famous family, the DeMedicis, of which more will be written hereafter.

Clement VII wished to stifle the heresies of Luther, but his followers had increased to such an extent, that all his efforts were unavailing. A war soon after broke out between the Pope and Charles V. Charles, with an army of Spanish Catholics, (who were opposed to Clement,) and German Lutherans. They sacked Rome, and committed all manner of cruelties. The Lutherans, as if revenging their own persecutions, and forgetting all mercy, were more cruel than the others; laid waste the Churches and Monasteries; they fell upon the houses of rich citizens, and mere artisans. They tore the nuns from their retreats and outraged them in the public square; women and young girls who had sought asylum in the sanctuaries and temples, were violated even there. Many men were submitted to most frightful tortures. Then, after they got tired of rapine, murder and plunder of the living, the Lutherans turned their attention to the graves of the dead; the tombs of the Popes were especially profaned; they clothed themselves in the sacredotal vestments, travestied themselves into Priests, Bishops and Cardinals; mounted the head of one of their number with a tiara taken from a dead body, placed him on an ass, and led him through the streets; then went to the Vatican and proclaimed Luther Sovereign Pontiff, amid acclamations so deafening that they were heard by Clement, who, from the towers of San. Angelo was coldly contemplating the disasters his oppresion and avarice had brought upon Rome.

In Germany, these so-called Reformers, moved by religious fanaticism, pursued the sect of Anabaptists with the utmost rigor, and exercised toward them the most frightful cruelties. It is said, by several historians, that no sect ever underwent martyrdom and torture with so much calmness and composure, as the Anabaptists. The most delicate females even, sought the most horrible torture, to show the strength of their faith.

We have no account of the doctrines of this remarkable sect, except such as is given us by their persecutors; aye, their executioners. As near as can be gathered from these, they were a species of communists, holding their property in common; they were accused without any direct proof however, of being immoral in their practices. This accusation does not sound very well, coming from the Mother of Harlots, or from the freeloving Lutherans, who forced nuns in the streets of Rome. It is seen by this history, that the Lutherans, in their turn, were most bitter persecutors, and cruel torturers, and many of them guilty of the most revolting immorality; in character a fit set to form the first horn on the head of the Old Beast.

After the sack of Rome, the Pope was kept in confinement six months; then the crafty King Charles released him, not without an object, which was to prevent, if possible, the divorce of Henry VIII King of England, from Catherine, who was his aunt.

The Pope then found himself between two fires, not wishing to offend either monarch; for the time had now come when the Pope trembled before Kings, instead of Kings before the Pope and Cardinals, as in the time of Gregory VII, and the Borgias.

Henry divined the secret motive of the Pope, and in order to force him to declare between him and Charles, he threatened to withdraw from the Church of Rome.

The Pope finally decided against Henry, who had secretly married Anne Boleyn, which coming to the knowledge of the Pope, he fulminated a terrible bull against this King. Henry tore up the Pontifical bull, and declared the English Church independent, and himself the head of the Church. (The history of this Church will be given in another Chapter).

While these events were taking place in England, the Pontiff conducted his niece, the infamous Catherine de Medicis, into France. She, though scarce fourteen years of age, had been initiated into the most infamous debaucheries; she was married to the son of Francis I.

It is related that after the nuptial ceremonies had been performed, Clement gave the young couple his benediction, saying: "Go and multiply."

Brantome, the historian of gallant anecdotes, relates the following adventure, which took place during a visit of the Pope to Marseilles: "The ladies of three provinces presented a request to the Duke of Albania, to obtain permission not to be deprived of meat during lent. This Lord feigned not to understand them, and introduced them to his Holiness, saying: "Most Holy Father, I present to you three young ladies, who desire to have the privilege of keeping company with men during lent. They beseech you to grant their requests."

Clement immediately raised them up, kissed them, and said, laughing: "What you ask is not most edifying, I however authorize you to do so three times a week, which is enough for the sin of luxury."

The ladies blushed, cried out, and explained to his Holiness that what they had solicted was a dispensation to allow them to eat flesh during lent; at which the Pope laughed heartily, kissed them again, and dismissed them."

Alexander Farness succeeded him as Paul III. He was accused of having made his daughter Constance his mistress! of having committed incest with his sister Wilhelmina, whom he had prostituted to Alexander VI. He was a man of considerable learning, and a great astrologer; regulated all his movements by the motions of the planets. He taught that the religion of the Catholic Church was identical with that of the ancient Persians, and Mithra and Jesus were the same God. He finally proclaimed himself a priest of the Sun, and proclaimed Sabeism. We have this on the authority of Mendoza.

This Pope occupied himself during the absence of his legates, in pushing nepotism further than any former Pope.

He gave a Cardinal's Hat to a youth of sixteen, the fruit of his amours with his daughter Constance; and bestowed like favors on several other bastards and minions. He declared Henry of England deprived of his throne, and all his children born or to be born of Anne Boleyn, bastards. This did not influence the King in the slightest degree; even after Anne was beheaded, he still continued his deadly enmity to the Church of Rome, though the Pope condescended to address him a special letter, exhorting him to return to the bosom of the Church.

But more terrible to the Pope than the contempt of Henry, was the appearance, about this time, of a work called "The Christian Institutions," which attacked not only the premacy of the See of Rome, but the authority of the General Council, Bishops and Priests; the author even rejected the necessity of baptism and communion, for the safety of men. This man, who had just placed himself at the head of a new sect, was John Calvin. He also exposed the doctrines and practices of the French Protestants; and attacked especially King Francis, and exposed his hipocrisy.

At the same time there was forming, in the dark, a deadly society, that was secretly striving to exterminate the Protestants; whose secret plans, for years moulded the politics of Catholic Europe, and even to this day, have their emmissaries all over the world: the terrible order of Jesuits, which was yet to envelope the world in its thousand cords, clasp thousands in its hideous embrace, and cause oceans of blood to flow. Its founder, Ignatius Loyola, was the descendant of an old Spanish family. He followed the army for a time until he broke a limb, which lamed him for life; after that, he practiced great austerity, and pretended to have visions; he averred that the Devil appeared to him, and was about to seize upon him, when the Virgin Mary appeared and put him to flight. Finally, his madness reached its height; he sold all his property, allowed his beard and nails to grow, soiled his face with filth, and went begging; he afterward went into a cave, where he remained eight days without recognizing any one, plunged in a profound lethargy; when he returned to life, he said angels had carried him to Heaven, he had seen the Trinity and the Holy Virgin—the Savior had ordered him to return to earth and form a secret Society for the perpetuation of the faith.

Thus commenced with the visions of a mendicant, that order that was one day to make Popes and Kings bow and tremble with fear. They were given full power to increase their numbers, and the influence they had over the strong mind of Pope Paul was very great; but this Pontiff at last had to go the way of all flesh; frightful ulcers were eating him up; and several painful operations had already been performed upon him. The dying man lost none of his great strength of mind, though he perceived his life was ebbing away. He showed he had no faith in his religion, for he daily consulted majicians, (mediums), astrologers, &c., upon his destiny, and those of his families. He died 1549.

A minion of his succeeded him, as Julius III. He was, according to Bayle, "a true soldier of ecclesiastical fortune. Gifted with a handsome person, it is easy to imagine what had procured him such high dignities. His language and manners were in keeping with the dissoluteness of his morals—even in the conclave he practiced beastiality of the most disgusting description; and instead of concealing it, allowed his colleagues to detect him."

Bayle has also preserved a correspondence between His Holiness and a courtezan of Rome, whose favors Julius shared with Cardinal Crecentius. These letters contain recitals so disgusting that we cannot put them in decent language. At Court, says a grave historian, "the days and nights were spent in feasting and saturnalia. It frequently happened, that the Pope, after getting intoxicated in company with his Cardinals and loose women, threw off his garments, compelled his guests, male and female, to do the same, then put on a sort of under vest, that scarcely came to the waist, and led this motley crew in dance around the gardens of the Vatican.

His Holiness was almost always drunk, and spent his nights in orgies with courtezans."

Nothing can give an exact idea of the gross impurity of this Pope. One night, in the midst of a debauch, he elevated his monkey keeper, Bertucino, to the rank of Cardinal. The Pope was drunk, and opened the assembly with a strange speech, in which he lauded the lascivious allurements of his minion; this created a lively opposition, at which the Pope swore by the Holy Virgin, "his minion should be Cardinal."

While the people of Italy were trying to free themselves from the tyranny of the Bishops, the Protestants (Calvinists) of Geneva became in their turn persecutors, and were erecting in a Public Square of their city the funeral pile that was to consume Michael Servetus, because he believed unbaptized infants could be saved; who was persecuted and condemned by both Lutherans and Calvinists. He was tried and found guilty of heresy by several judges, but none saw fit to pronounce upon him the sentence of death.

But finally, on Oct. 26, 1555, the Tribunal of Two Hundred yielding to *the urgent solicitations of Calvin, condemned him to be burned alive.* When the sentence was made known to Servetus, he asked to see Calvin, and had an interview of two hours with him; but strove in vain to wake within his heart a single sentiment of pity. *Nothing could assuage the dogged will of this so-called Reformer.*

The death of Servetus shows that the great Protestant Oracle, Calvin, like his Catholic predecessors, was ignorant of the true principles of justice and mercy, and adds another link in the great chain of proof of the corrupting influence of creeds, and the corruption of creed makers.

When the soul becomes bound to opinion, and wishes to rivet the some fetters on its fellow beings, it naturally sets in motion all the bad qualities of its nature, and leads the individual to think he is doing God service by torturing those who are so unfortunate as to hold different opinions, and bow down before other Gods.

Such a spirit is the legitimate parent of immorality, bloodshed, and every sort of crime.

Protestantism became the established religion of Germany about this time. When the knowledge of this came to Julies III, it threw him into a violent passion, which caused his death March 23, 1555.

Paul IV, a most cruel and execrable Pontiff, was noted for his vindictive disposition, from his earliest years. He was a great friend to the Jesuits; he renewed with vigor the religious persecutions, and lit again the flames of the *au-to-da-fe*. During his reign the follwing terrible event occurred in France, says Mazerai:

"On one night in autumn, the Jesuits were informed that about two hundred persons of the reformed religion of Calvin, were praying together in a private hotel in the Fauburg St. Germain; they, (the Jesuits,) collected a crowd before the house, crying scandal, abomination.

The worshippers, alarmed by the yells of their enemies wished to fly; before they could do so, the doors were broken in, and more than a hundred were arrested and dragged to the dungeons of the city.

The disciples of Loyola became their accusers, and produced accusations against them as strange as false. "They asserted that the Calvinists roasted young children, and ate their flesh at their horrid repasts, after which, men and women, in the obscurity of the night, mixed in the most horrible embraces."

These calumnies sent a large number of Protestants to the stake.

How much this resembles the false accusations of these same Calvinists and other orthodox sects, preferred against the reformers now, calling them Atheists, Freelovers, etc., guilty of all kinds of Immoralities—all of which are without a shadow of foundation in fact.

Let the would-be Jesuits of this age of Protestant America, learn a lesson from the past, and what it has given, and strive to profit by the present and its Living Gospel. Then will the spirit of persecution leave them, never more to return. On the death of Paul IV, his dead body was placed on a hurdle, dragged through the streets of Rome, and then cast into a sink.

Pius IV, his successor, as soon as he was consecrated, showed himself greedy of gold and power, cruel and debauched, even surpassing his predecessor in perfidy and crimes. He was very avaricious in all matters except gluttony. With all his taste for licentiousness, he managed to possess the handsomest women and youth of Rome, without costing him anything. He would make them large presents, till he got them in his power, then put them to the torture to make them return them. He sent Jesuits into all the Courts of Europe, to engage Catholic Princes to form a league for the extermination of heretics. The league was formed, and the soldiers were mustered, among them were many priests, monks, etc. The soldiers of the Pope, says Varillas, "marked their passage through Provence, by all kinds of depredations and cruelties, (including murders and other most heinous crimes.) They spared however, all the she goats, which they used in their debaucheries. The goat of the General had gilded horns. This band of wretches fell on the small city of Orange, and carried it by assault—then were committed crimes, the recital of which is enough to make the hair rise erect, and the blood curdle—they put men, women and children to the most frightful torture, hung them on hooks over slow fires, put long poles into their bodies, tore out their entrails, and violated young girls."

Finally, these satellites of Pontifical tyranny, assuaged their lubricity on young boys scarce ten years of age, then fastened them to racks, and larded them with leaves of protestant bibles, as you would the flesh of birds."

In the meantime, the execrable Pius, at Rome, regaled himself by day with the punishments in the halls of the Inquisition, and by night plunged into drunken debauches with his mistresses, favorites and minions. One night, after drinking twelve flasks of wine, he was taken with apoplexy and died, Dec. 1565.

Pius V, was another of the same stamp, was violent in his persecutions of all heretics; his wrath was particularly kindled against the

Hugenots. Although the Catholic soldiers were very cruel, the Pope reproved the Marshal severely for saving a single one of a conquered army alive.

"In the name of Christ, (said he in a letter to the King of France) I order you to hang or behead the prisoners you have made, without regard to learning, rank, sex or age, without human respect or pity."

This was accordingly done under the superintendence of a Jesuit named Babelot. This wretch had the cruelty to trample little children under his feet, to have the females violated, and then murder them himself; the men he had flayed alive, and then burned. In Venice, the Jesuits were in great honor, and had it not been for their ardor in confessing women and girls in their private apartments, they might have maintained it; but this drew on them the hatred of the Senators; and the Doge having learned that his wife went to confession three times in one day, it was decided they should be expelled from the territory.

In the dominion of Savoy, they had seized on all employments, and could with impunity violate women, or use young boys for their infamous pleasures. The sanguinary monster, Pius, according to the historian DeThou, "had improved in the refinements of punishment, on the fabulous ferocity of Procustes and Gergian." That Pope who had the execrable glory of surpassing the atrocity of the Neros; that executioner of humanity; that murderer of women, children and old men; that organizer of the most frightful plot that ever alarmed the world; of that St. Bartholomew, which, four months after, covered France with a hundred thousand corpses, has found Priests, who have made a saint of him, who have canonized him, have held him up as an example for the Kings of Europe. This terrible massacre took place during the Pontificiate of Gregory XIII. It was finally brought about by the treachery of this Holy Father and the infamous Catharine de Medecis. After the bloody deed was accomplished, the Holy Father received the news thereof with inexpressible joy; he caused the cannon in the castle of San Angelo to be fired, and commanded public rejoicings, to celebrate the triumph of the holy cause, and then published a jubilee through all Europe, in order, he said, "that the

Catholics might rejoice with their head, at that magnificent holoicaust offered to the Papacy by the King of France."

Catherine de Medecis sent the Pope the head of **Admiral Coligny**, leader of the Hugenots. Brantome says: "It was the head of that Admiral, which the mother and son (Catherine and Charles,) those crowned murderers, had sundered from his noble body and sent to the Pope, as the most agreeable offering they could **send to the Vicar of Christ**." Gregory received it with transports of ferocious joy. This terrible wretch died of apoplexy, while preparing a **terrible bull** against the remnant of the Hugenots; having given an example of every vice in the world.

Sixtus V was noted for his cold, implacable cruelty, his amours and persecutions. He wished, however, to reform the Jesuits, and sent a committee of investigation to inquire into the progress, wealth and morality of this secret order. Cardinal Aldobrandin, the head of this committee, declared, "that they could not find one monastery in Italy, where the religious devotees were not addicted to drunkenness, sodomy, and all kinds of abominations." "They reported that in Austria, they had visited 122 convents of men, and had counted in the monasteries of monks, 199 prostitutes, and 55 boys and girls, of less than twelve years of age; and in the houses of the nuns, 443 male domestics, who were at once the servants and lovers of the sisterhood; and in France, the convents were the theatres of still greater outrages, and cited among others, the monks of Aurillac. It was proved that several of these monks had as many as **five or six mistresses at** once, either courtezans, or young girls carried off from their parents, or women suborned or ravished from their husbands; that they had, moreover, a large number of bastards, whom they used as minions; it was also proved that the Abbot Charles de Senectarie, made sorties at the head of his monks, beat up the country to find maidens, and drove before him with his cross, in open day, such as suited, and forced them to enter his den, without the father and mother being able to offer the least resistance, from fear of being assassinated by the monks. It resulted from these depositions, that the monastery was secularized." This Pope finally died, poisoned by the Jesuits, Aug.

27, 1590; this was also the fate of Urban VII, who succeeded him. Next came Clement VIII, who terminated worthily the series of Popes of the sixteenth century.

Step by step they had disputed the ground of their spiritual and temporal omnipotence, step by step, by force and ruses, deceit, crime, and outrage, the blood red hand of open murder, and the subtle poison of the Borgias. Paul V, the first Pontiff of the next century, was noted for his nepotism and incests, Gregory XV, and his nephew Ludovico, next ruled Rome and her surroundings. The latter was a notorious debauchee, and historical facts show that Gregory equalled in ferocity his predecessors. They say he was better as a man than as a Pope, and one of his worst faults was a desire to promote his relatives at any cost of life and treasure. The subtle Barberino, who ascended the Papal Chair as Urban VIII, was bad enough to be placed with the most infamous Pontiffs. When the Cardinals assembled to elect a Pope, he organized a gang of banditti, under whose ravages Rome became the theatre of frightful barbarities; the bravos of the Cardinal pillaged houses, murdered old men and children, violated women and young girls, and frightfully profaned their dead bodies; and when satiated with carnage and licentiousness, ran through the streets with torches crying, "Death and fire, or Pope Barberino!" which cry reached the ear of the assembled Cardinals, and chilled them with terror. Daily, one by one of the opposers of the wretch, died suddenly, and it became evident to all, that he was ridding himself of enemies by poison. This so frightened the survivors, that they at once elected him Pope. It was during his reign that the wise Galileo, after inventing the telescope, and affirming that the world turned round, was thrown into Prison, put to the torture, and made to abjure the truths he had deduced from nature. He wished them to examine his works, and look through the telescope—but no, said Pope Urban, "By virtue of my infallibility, I declare the earth is immovable, and governed by laws pointed out in Genesis." How like the bigots now, who refuse to investigate new laws of mind, and say spirits cannot come back anyway, therefore we will not investigate, and you are a fool for believing it. There are many Pope Urbans now, who would make us abjure the things we know, *if they could.* But even if they had the power so to do, it would be knowledge still, as Galileo said of the world, "*E si per muove,*" (it moves still).

While this persecution was going on at Rome, in France, royalty was still trampling under foot the rights of humanity. Those who incurred the wrath of Cardinal Richelieu or the Jesuits, were inveighed against as sorcerers, and accused of all manner of absurd and impossible crimes. On one occasion the young Princess Catherine de Loraine, was attacked with a lingering illness, and forthwith one of the enemies of the Jesuits was put to torture, and finally death, for having put a spell on her. After his death they began to exorcise the Princess. The exorcist, who was a Jesuit Priest, demanded to be left alone with the princess all night, in order as he said, to perform his ceremonies without being disturbed. But the young lady's father, curious to see the process, watched one night, and found them asleep in each other's arms. His anger was so great that he strangled the monk on the spot, and to clear himself asserted that he (the monk) had fallen in strife with an evil spirit. He was afterward canonized by petition of the Jesuits. Well was he worthy to be a patron saint of that cruel and licentious order.

The Jesuits had a multitude of curious and scandalous laws, that sanctioned every kind of immorality and crime. We will only quote a few of their freelove maxims, to show the condition of their morals. 1st. "It is not a great sin for young girls to abandon themselves to love before marriage, nor for women to receive the embraces of other men, and be unfaithful to their husbands, under certain circumstances. 2d. A man and a woman who are strangers, may unrobe in the presence of each other, even to the last garment, without committing sin. A young woman may, without sinning, be particular in her attire, in order to promote the carnal desires of man, and wear fine and delicate garments, which show her bosom or the contour of her limbs, provided the world permits it. 3d. A man does not commit sin, be he monk or priest even, who having gone to a place of debauchery, to talk morality to harlots, though he should succumb to temptation, even though he had frequently proved his liability to be seduced by women of love; the intention which led him there, is enough to preserve him from sin.

4th. Robbery is not a sin under certain circumstances, a woman may, unknown to her husband, take from the common purse as much as she may judge necessary for *pious donations;* she may steal to spend at her leisure, whether in play, on her toilet, or even to pay her lovers *provided she gives half to the Church.*

5th. If a monk, though well informed of the danger he runs in being surprised in adultery, enters armed into the house of the woman he loves, and kills her husband in defense of his life, it is not irregular, and he may continue his ecclesiastical functions."

These are but a fraction of the ridiculous code of Jesuitical morals. All crimes were sanctioned, provided the criminal would give half the spoils to the Church; then they would assist him, no matter how guilty, only the greater the crime, the more the pay. Urban VIII breathed his last, blaspheming the name of God, and confounding in the same curses both Protestants and Catholics. He was followed by Innocent X, whose incestuous amours with his sister-in-law, Donna Olympia, are matters of history. This crafty woman was the virtual ruler of the Church. She married his son Camilla to another Olympia, who disputed the price of infamy with her mother-in-law. Frightful quarrels broke out between these two women, which filled Rome with scandal. He afterward took active part in all the intrigues of the palace, and by turns elevated to power, or hurled from it, the creatures of his sister and daughter-in-law, as either succeeded over her rival, and merited the preference of the old cynic, by lascivious caresses, or infamous compliances. He gave the post of Datary of the Roman Church, to the lover of the young Olympia, in recompense for her having given him a spectacle of women entirely naked, abandoning themselves to the games of the courtezans of Lesbos; he then disgraced this favorite, to give his post to a lover of his sister-in law, who had regained her empire over him by surpassing the shameful orgies of the other. Donna Olympia the older, finally prepared her own disgrace, by the very means by which she was trying to make her power more lasting, she persuaded the Pope to adopt as Cardinal nephew, a handsome young man, a lover of hers; the Pope was so captivated by his beauty, that he made him his minion. He afterwards became the lover of the younger Olympia, and the elder was buried in disgrace for remonstrating with the Pope. She was finally restored, and was with him at the time of his death, Jan. 5, 1655.

Alexander VII, according to Guiacomo Quirni, "thought of nothing but wallowing in the mire of licentiousness." He died in 1667, and went to join in eternity, the execrable Pontiffs who had preceded him. Clement X was a miserable, drunken wretch, over eighty years old when he became Pope. He finally died from the effects of dissipation.

During the reign of Innocent XII, there appeared in France a singular woman, named Jeanne Guyon, who had wonderful visions, and in connection with a monk called Father Lacombe created great sensation wherever they were known. The Church commenced persecuting them, of course—they taught many singular and foolish doctrines, and among them some beautiful truths. She afterward made the acquaintance of Fenelon, and a tender liason between the ardent quietist Jeanne, and this wise Abbot, commenced. The latter, says St. Simon, "was for a long time addicted to a refined spiritualism, tested the doctrines of Jeanne, and affirmed she was one of the most sublime of Saints." This inoffensive spiritual female was brought before the tribunal, and made to abjure her so called heresies; and to the eternal shame of Bosuet be it spoken, he was among the chief of her persecutors.

This brings us to the eighteenth century, when the decline of the Papal Power, and the rule of Priests over the minds of the people, slowly but surely begins to be made tangibly manifest. A class of men arose in this age, who feared not man, the dogmas of the Church or the bans of a depraved priesthood. This was the age of Paine, Voltaire, and that other host of philosophical thinkers, whom the world has branded as infidels; but who really did more toward overthrowing or modifying the Papal Power than all the Protestants ever have done, or in their present condition ever can do. The master spirits of the French revolution, with a sublime purpose before them, strove to make France free from temporal and spiritual despotism. They failed, because the people were not prepared for freedom, and designing men placed themselves at the head of Government, and the reign of terror commenced. The infidels were not to blame for this, but the tyrants who had oppressed and ground down the people for ages; and when they were let loose, there was no bounds to their rapacity; like a wild beast, who is kept weeks chained, and half starved, and then let loose to gorge itself at leisure.

Such was the condition of the oppressed, after the death of Louis XVI. Is it then to be wondered at that the French revolution was a sublime failure, even as the American was a holy triumph of freedom's cause?

Clement XI, was the first Pope of this century. During his Pontificiate, Rome was visited by a famine, and a pestilence; many starved to death, and many more were compelled to prostitute their wives and daughters to the Priests and Bishops, who were alone rich enough to procure food. Says the historian: "It was at once an afflicting and humiliating spectacle, to behold the dwellings of Priests turned into seraglios, in which were to be found the youngest and handsomest girls in Rome."

They plunged into such excess, that the Holy Father issued a bull forbidding them from practicing licentiousness, or to get drunk while Rome was in distress, and to immediately restore to their friends the girls they had taken. Whether they obeyed or not, we have no means of knowing. On the death of Clement, Pasquin made his funeral eulogy in two lines, as follows:

"Rome rejoice! thou art delivered from that Pope, who promised much, performed but little, and wept all the time."

Benedict XII, was, according to Father Cloche, "of a character so detestable, that he resembled a club of accasia, pointed, hard and crooked." During his reign the Jesuits began to intrigue to have the famous Monk, Hildebrand, the poisoner of Popes, him, who, by the name of Gregory VII had exalted the religious power, trampled under foot Kings and Emperors, canonized. The Pope consented, but it was too great a pill to go down with the French people; they refused to sanction it, or credit the legends in connection therewith. Another miserable debauchee, Pius VI, ascended the Papal Chair in 1774. His election was brought about by the wiles of courtezans, who influenced the assembled Cardinals to vote for whoever they should designate. His morals were awful, and his administration cruel and malignant throughout.

Gorain, author of the secret memoirs of Italy, a work of high historical importance, accuses him formally of "adultery, incest and sodomy." All cotemporary authors, except the stipendiaries of the Jesuits, agree in saying, "that this Holy Father led the life of a sybarite, passing his time in getting drunk with his mistresses and minions who were chosen from his own family."

The intolerence and cupidity of this Pope, and the arrogant oppression of the King and Court of France, were the legitimate cause of that uprising of the people in that terrible revolution that deluged the Nation with blood and carnage. The Pope imposed the most dreadful punishment on all revolutionists that fell in his power. All through his life he continued hating and being hated, alike despised and execrated by all good men, he ended his infamous and bloody career Aug. 29, 1799, and was the last Pope of the century. A fit finale to this chapter of awful cruelties, persecution and crime.

The nineteenth century was the dawn of a new era. Bonaparte was then Consul, and by his influence Pius VII was chosen Pope. The time had now come when the Papal Power trembled before that man of destiny, who was yet to make the empires of all Europe shake. This Pope was ever the willing servant of Napoleon, and went to France to crown him when he became Emperor. This great man had he lived and still conquered, would have sounded the death knell of the Papal Power, and proclaimed religious freedom throughout Europe. But he fell in the height of his glory, and the coward Bourbons came to prostrate themselves in abject servitude at the gates of Rome. But such was the fatality of France, to loose her greatest benefactor, and be trampled under foot anew by the minions of the Pope. This Pontiff at last died April 23, 1823. Leo XII succeeded him. During his reign the last *au-to-da-fee* took place, ever celebrated in Spain.

He was a great friend to the Jesuits, and all other tyrants who served his will.

Gregory XVI, according to those who ought to know, was a very immoral man; he was openly designated as the father of seven children, by the beautiful Cajatanina, and in the upper circles of the city an anecdote is related of a young nurse of Tivoli, remarkably handsome, who had for a short time attracted the attention of His Holiness. The conduct of this Pope was publicly blamed. He died very suddenly, some say not without help, by poison.

Pius IX, the present Pontiff was his successor. We will leave it for future historians to give the character of this Holy Father, of his cowardice and Jesuitical diplomacy. Of his intrigues for power in America, by means of Jesuitical Nuncios, wandering Priests, and other vassals; his servile fear during the last Italian wars, and the massacre, by his order, of the peaceable inhabitants of Perugia. The Pope is still the same as in former years; like his predecessors he has been cruel and ambitious. His submission to Louis Napoleon reminds us strikingly of the rule of Napoleon I, over Pius VII.

The Italians hoped much from the last war, and gained but little; although the power of the Pope is weakened, it is not destroyed; and his is the power beyond all others, that tramples Italy under the feet of a most terrible despotism.

The time for her freedom is not yet come. Of what avail is her beautiful climate and balmy air, her beautiful hills and fertile valleys, her olive groves and rich laden vines, her lovely sky, and all those golden features that make her the land of poesy and song, while her aspiring sons and beauteous daughters are but the vassals of the Papal Power?

Behold the influence of Priestcraft! look at Italy, there is an example. Naught else to hinder it from being one of the loftiest nations on earth, save that satanic power, which under the name and guise of religion, has for ages crushed the holiest rights and most sacred privileges of the people. Oh, descendants of the Cæsars and Scipios! you, in whose veins flow the blood of Petrarch and Tasso! ye, whose souls are filled with poetry and song, arise and assert the dignity of your manhood, and be free! Yes, we feel that the time must come, when this nation will arise and take its place among the foremost of earth. For there is a time when this great Church will be obliged to release its victims, and let its oppressed children be free.

We have now traced in brief, the history of the Catholic Church from its earliest years up to the present time, with a view to examine candidly and impartially the moral character of its leading men. Inasmuch as christianity is said to promote morality, it was thought the truth or falsity of that assertion could be best proved by historical facts. The reader of these pages will perceive, that so far it *has not* been productive of high toned morality, even in the life of its holy Vicars on earth. And all the vast machinery of the Catholic Church has been only a great puzzling chain, to deceive the people, place on their necks the yoke of temporal and spiritual bondage, and made them give up their substance and persons to the will of a few designing men, many of whom despised the very religion they taught, only as it was a means of personal aggrandizement or passional gratification. This is not only true of the Catholic, which is the mother of all the other Churches, but in a degree with all creed makers. We have shown that Lutherans, Calvinists and other Protestants, as soon as they got a little power, were, under the same circumstances, as cruel as the Catholics.

These were the first dissenting sects, and the parents of most modern Protestant denominations. A step in advance of the old Church we admit, for this is a world of progress, but a very short step. The natural tendency of all religious chains is to retard the progress of humanity, not to advance it. Hence you see the so called religion of past and present times, always opposed to improvements, scientific, political, social and religious reform, and ever prating about the world's deterioration, and lamenting the days of greater power that are passed and gone forever.

CHAPTER VI.

PROTESTANTISM; THE ENGLISH CHURCH, HENRY VIII, ITS FATHER. THE PURITANS, THEIR CHARACTER. A GLANCE AT ALL THE PROTESTANT CHURCHES; HAVE THEY A HIGH-TONED MORALITY?

The English Church had no influence as a body, till after the separation of Henry VIII from the Roman See. There were a few scattered Protestants in England, as in other portions of Europe, but they had very little influence in moulding the affairs of State. The Episcopalians claim that they are the primitive Church, and that their Bishops have followed the Apostles in regular succession; same as Catholics reckon St. Peter as their first Pope; and with not as much show of truth; for all reliable history shows, that the Catholic Church, so far as age is concerned, is superior to any other. Henry VIII, because the Pope would not consent to his divorce from Catherine of Aragon, that he might wed the young and beautiful Anne Boleyn, separated himself from the mother Church, and declared the English Church independent. Look at the object! he had been a zealous persecutor of the few Protestants that fell within his power; but religion, with him, was an indifferent affair in comparison to the gratification of his low, sensual desires. So far as his practical freeloveism was concerned he would have made a very good Pope. It is useless to give his history at length in these pages, for his name is familiar to everybody, as representing England's vilest King. The sensuality, cruelty and oppression of this haughty monarch is known to every schoolboy— how he caused the unfortunate Anne Boleyn to be beheaded, in a fit of jealousy; how he divorced Anne of Cleves, because she was not suited to his taste; how his fifth wife, Catherine Howard met the same fate as Anne Boleyn, and from the same cause. His sixth wife was so fortunate as to outlive the monster, who was about preparing the means of her ruin or death. He was filled with a loathesome disease, and she watched and cared for him as if he had been her patron saint instead of a vile, dissolute old King, who was ready to cause her death any moment the whim should strike him. This monarch is shown up as a vile character, by all historians, and his memory is execrated by all good people at the present time. Still, he was the father of the English Church. Had he not braved the Catholic Power, and married Anne Boleyn, England might now, perhaps, or at least for a long time after that, been the vassal of the Papal Power, as is Ireland now. The people would not then have dared to rise and assert their views. More than this, Elizabeth, that defender of the Church of England, would not have had being, (she was daughter of Anne Boleyn) had it not been for this bold stroke of Henry. We must then state the facts, however cutting they may be to the Episcopalians of this country, and say their Church owes its origin to the freeloveism of a King. This Church is superior in every respect to the Catholic, yet the difference is slight; their articles of faith are very much the same. One believes in the supremacy of the Pope, and worships the Virgin Mary; the other does not. One reads service in Latin; the other in English. One reckons the succession from St. Peter, the other from St. Paul. These constitute the principal differences we are able to discover; though the latter sanctions the marriage of their priesthood, which inculcates a superior morality to the doctrine of celibacy, taught, (not practiced) by the Catholics. The Church of England was not fairly organized in the time of Henry, but during the reign of his son, Edward VI, it was fully established, and the litany which is now in use, was then adopted. It received a check in the bloody reign of Queen Mary, whose cruelties to all Protestants are well known. In the time of Elizabeth, the religion of Episcopacy became fully incorporated into the National Government. She labored zealously for its union and strength. She was a good Queen, so far as governing the masses was concerned, and the common people always spoke of her as good Queen Bess; but she was cross and irascible to her friends, would even box the ears of those around her in her sallies of anger, no matter what their rank or station. She was never married, but had a great many favorites, prominent among whom was the Earl of Leicester and the Earl of Essex. Leicester was a notorious villain, but the Queen was much attached to him, and it was for a long time thought she would marry him; he had a lovely young wife whom he had married secretly, and it is generally believed that she was murdered by his orders, in order that she might not stand between him and the Queen. This man was very intimate with Elizabeth, as also was Essex; who, half insane, at last tried to get up a rebellion in London, which was of course the means of his death. Elizabeth cherished for him a romantic fondness, even to her old age, and after his death she sank into a profound melancholy, which continued till the time of her death. Elizabeth had a great many good qualities which we would by no means undervalue, but if she had lived at the present time, she would certainly have been called a freelover. Her persecution of and cruelty to the unfortunate Mary, Queen of Scots, whom she kept in confinement eighteen years, and then caused to be executed on a charge of conspiracy, shows that the religion of which she was such a zealous advocate, had not taught her a single lesson of mercy or toleration. James, who succeeded her, weak minded King though he was, was pious enough to persecute the Puritans, and force a large number of them to leave the country, or renounce their religion. They chose the former, and came to the (then) wilderness of America, to found a new colony. Charles I, who was still more bitter in his persecutions, succeeded him. His advocacy of the high Church, and his rigorous measures with regard to all other sects, drew on him the hatred of a large class of people. He issued an order, forbidding the Puritans from leaving England, and drew on himself the resentment of the whole Scottish nation, by attempting to make the people of that country conform to the rules of the Church of England. But the people at length arose, and beheaded this tyrant. The Dictator Cromwell governed the country well till the time of his death. Charles 2d, a good High Churchman, who distinguished himself by his persecutions of all dissenters from Episcopacy, was a shameless profligate, who did not scruple to betray the national interests, honor, and even religion, for money to squander in his debaucheries. He was a reckless and dissolute man, through all his life. These are some of the fathers and mothers of the Church of England; the most powerful of Protestant Churches, and the first step, so far as ceremonies are concerned, from the Roman Church. They were wanting in morality, then why are we to be called upon to receive their dogmas? If these dogmas, in themselves, contained the elements of morality, surely their first founders would have partaken in a measure, of that purity. Not so, however—still another link is added to our chain of proof, showing that forms, in themselves, are unavailing. The dissoluteness of these old English Kings and Queens, is a matter of history, and cannot be gainsayed. We would ask the Episcopalians of this country, many of whom we respect for their integrity and worth, (though we do not acknowledge their religion as the cause o their goodness) how they account for the immorality of their ancestors? Here are the facts, readers may draw their own conclusions The Episcopalian Church of America, has also had its delinquents. and occasionally ejects members for immorality. Not many years ago in one of our principal cities a Bishop was deposed for being a practical freelover. How is this to be accounted for? only on the hypothesis that churchmen are no better than the rest of mankind. A few years ago, a well-known Episcopal Clergyman at A. in this State (Michigan) decamped with his servant girl. These are but few of the great multitude of incidents of this kind, occuring all the while. But shall we blame for that those of the Church who are truly pure and good? by no means; we only criticise the creeds under which men take these licenses. We also wish to remind those of this and other sects, who are continually boasting of their purity, and condemning those who differ with them in opinion, as guilty of all kinds of impurity, that it would be well for them to look at their own flock, and see if there are not some whose morals need looking after, quite as much as the spiritualists, and others, whom they are daily accusing. The Puritans, who were before alluded to, as being driven out of England by the persecution of Kings and rulers, were a sect who ignored all Bishops and religious rulers, except the creed of their particular Church. Every Church was, and is now, with them an absolute monarchy of itself, or rather, an independent theocracy. This constitutes the principal difference between them and the Presbyterians, their belief being about the same. These Puritans came to America, then a wild and unsettled region, for "freedom to worship God," freedom for themselves only, for no sooner did they get firmly planted on the rocks of New England, than they began to make the most cruel and oppressive laws possible, and show the most bitter intolerance to all other sects. The brave, heroic and pious Roger Williams, was one of the first victims to their vindictive spirit. He was banished from Salem for his heresies, and settled near what is now Providence, R. I. where he founded a colony. His spirit of toleration was too much for the bigoted Puritans, and he was obliged to fly for his life. Some of their persecuted ones did not come off as well as Old Roger—the Quakers, for instance, were particularly the subjects of the vengeance of these pious men; some were sold into slavery, or what is just the same, bound out to Puritan task masters; and many were hung; some on Boston common, and a tree is still standing there, on which a quaker woman was hung. The Salem witchcraft trials and executions took place under the auspices of these men of God. Twenty men and women were hung on various accusations, like the following:

Some asserted that they had seen black men, who looked like Indians, appear to them suddenly; that they seemed to walk in the air, and sometimes addressed them. Oh! that must be the Devil, anyway! said these brave soldiers *of the only true faith.* Some were accused of being seen riding broomsticks in the air, and of having teats between their fingers where little devils came and sucked. Others were accused of casting spells on people, and making them sick; and many other equally ridiculous and impossible things. If any one had an enemy, all he had to do was to accuse him or her of being a witch, and the person was sure to be imprisoned or put to death. Cotton Mather, a leading divine of that day, was one of the most zealous accusers of the so called bewitched ones. He led the committees of investigation, and was the most strenuous of any in advocating the severest punishment of all the bewitched. What a picture of the piety and morals of the early Puritans; these innocent men and women, because they saw black men, that looked like Indians, must needs be hung to appease divine wrath, or the private piques and revengeful desires of designing men and women against their neighbors, must be assisted by the strong arm of the law, and in the name of religion.

We would not be understood as denying all the phenomena of this Priest styled witchcraft; by no means. Spiritual agencies no doubt had something to do with the matter. The spirits of Indians, and other low, revengeful minds, seized this opportunity to enter and torment their enemies. The wise Puritans held fasts to drive out the Devil, but he would not obey them. They finally, (sagacious men) discovered that it was witchcraft, and one Mary Sibley was advised and disciplined for it.

One Martha Currier confessed that she was a witch, and paid the penalty of death therefor; her children also confessed they were witches. One Allen Toothaker testified that he was riding one day with one of these children, when he was prostrated by some unseen power; and when he recovered himself, he saw the spirit of Martha Currier pass over his breast. A woman also confessed that she had heard the voice of Martha many times. A companion of Martha confessed openly, that she had attended a witch meeting with her, and the Devil carried them through the air on broomsticks, which broke, and they fell to the ground. What could have induced them to give such evidence? If these manifestations had occurred in this age, spiritualists would know very well how to apply them, and instead of putting the unfortunate victims to death, who were thus possessed, they would have been treated kindly, and these low spirits either benefited or cast out

Observe one fact in this connection; not a single accusation is brought against the moral character of these witches. All the accusations are founded on that execrable law of Moses, "thou shalt not suffer a witch to live." It was the Puritan creed that was the means of the persecution of these unfortunates. If the mediums of this age had lived in the days of Cotton Mather, they would have shared the same fate. Our fathers, who were their judges, if they had gone to the right cause, would have put the halters about their own necks, for they had brought about this unnatural state of things by their own ignorance, bigotry and superstition. So much for the poor martyred witches; they are a continual source of accusation against the Puritan Church.

The Blue Laws of Connecticut, show up these old bigots, about as well as any record they have left behind them. The Sabbath laws in particular, are worthy of note. Not many years ago, stages and other public conveyances were not allowed to carry passengers on Sunday; every Sunday mail coach was regularly searched in every village by tithing men, and if a passenger was found therein on Sunday, he was stopped over till the next day, and both himself and the driver fined. Still further back in the old collonial times, "persons must not walk on the Sabbath, except to and from Church, in a quiet, orderlie manner. Mothers should not kiss their children Sundays. If friends come from afar in vessels, and landed Sunday, they should not be greeted with a kiss." Another ridiculous and oppressive law was made with regard to the hair. "No woman should on any account wear her hair croppiet like a man; no man shall wear his hair flowing on the shoulders, but croppiet round with the cap, and his face shall be properlie shaven. Women shall not uncover their heads in church."

It was then considered a sin to have stoves in Churches, even in the depth of the coldest New England winter; it was thought the people must be very depraved if their religion could not keep them warm. At that day every town had its stocks and whipping post; and every one who did not pay proper respect to these execrable laws, and more execrable men who made them, was publicly whipped or placed in these stocks; even females were sometimes thus exposed, to satisfy the vengeance of these elect of God. But it was no crime in their eyes to commit these barbarities, but an unpardonable sin not to believe little infants went to hell, and this terrible locality paved with the skulls of these little innocents who died unregenerated. It was there in Connecticut that the old "Saybrook Platform" was adopted, which is still the basis of all *Orthodox* creeds.

One article of faith teaches the unjust and unnatural doctrine of election; another the infernal dogma of infant damnation. Is it a wonder that old Puritans were cruel? How could they be otherwise with such a horrible belief? The creed book is the same now as then, but the natural progress of humanity has made the people better than their articles of faith, in spite of their determination to cling to the "good old platform." Were these terribly pious bigots all moral men? By no means—search the criminal records of those times, and you will find church members and even ministers have been found guilty (though very seldom punished) of adultery, seduction, and other scandalous crimes, with all their boasted piety. Even down to the present time, we scarcely take up a newspaper, without reading an account of the derelictions of some of their leading men.

With a glance at this and other denominations, as now existing, we will close this chapter. There are none perfect, neither should they be expected to be; but when men set themselves up as lights for the world to see by, we have a right to expect that they will at least *be full as good* as the rest of mankind.

The Baptist denomination professes to be very particular, will not commune even with other evangelical orders; they deem themselves the specially chosen ones of God, and look upon all others as inferior in point of religious development and purity. Yet there are freelovers among them, though they are most zealous in their persecutions of all reformers. There is not a week passes but that we hear of some dereliction of members of this sect. What an excitement was created a few years ago in Boston and vicinity, on account of the trial of Rev. J. H. F———. He was not convicted, though evidence was offered overwhelming and direct, by the girl herself, and corroborative testimony by others, that he was guilty of the crime of adultery; and illicit fatherhood. Rev. I. K——, in the same city, a short time since, was arraigned for the same crime, and the evidence was direct to the point; he was acquitted, *because the character of the witness was not good.* He is one of the most eloquent divines in the whole denomination. We mention these two, because they are men well known as leading men in their sect. If we were to write all the cases of freeloviem which have come to our knowledge in this sect alone, they would make a much larger book than this; we will narrate but a few. One case occurred in this State (Michigan) in Oakland County. A Baptist deacon, a wealthy man, and a leading member of the church, was proved to have offered violence to a young girl scarce thirteen years of age, who resided in his family. "Rev. Mr. Miner, of Donalsonville, Conn., lately confessed that for two years, (while he was pastor of the Baptist Church in that place) he had had criminal intercourse with a Mrs. R——, whom he had assisted to get a divorce from her husband, who was in California. When the husband returned, he attempted to kill the reverend rascal, but he escaped, and left for parts unknown, leaving a wife and two children." We clip the above from the Hartford Times of about Nov. 3, 1859; besides, we are personally acquainted with the facts, being in the vicinity when the event took place. One more, and we have done with this Church. An apparently respectable young man, who was a member of the Baptist Church, in good standing, and highly recommended by its Pastor, wooed and won a young lady, wealthy and accomplished, of good family and connections. They lived together about a year and a half, when he was detected in adultery with a servant girl; not only that, but it was proved that he kept daily company with prostitutes, and the lowest kind of street walkers; robbed his father-in-law of several thousand dollars, which he squandered in drunkenness and debauchery; more than this, he attempted to poison his wife, had even procured strychnine for the purpose. He was detected, and fled for his life; he was not sought for, or brought under the law, becase her friends did not wish to undergo the *horrid* publicity of such a trial. These are facts, ample proof of which is in our possession, and names, dates and places can be given to those who have a right to know.

About a year ago, one of the Congregational Churches in New Haven was occupied for a long time, in looking into several cases of alleged immorality, of which they found sufficient proof to warrant them in dealing with several. We copy from the New Haven Journal:

"One of the Churches in this city is engaged in investigating a lamentable charge of conjugal infidelity, involving the reputation of several church members, both male and female, and even assailing some of the highest dignitaries of the Church."

Another, we copy from the N. Y. Herald, with regard to a member of the Presbyterian sect, in Cincinnati:

"A NAUGHTY SUNDAY SCHOOL TEACHER.—A flour merchant in Cincinnati, who has for years been a rigid member of the Presbyterian Church, (outwardly at least) and a Sunday School teacher, was called before a justice a short time since, to answer to a charge of illicit fatherhood, preferred against him by a young woman, who swore point blank that he ruined her while she was under his own roof, taking care of his two small children." Another from the same paper:

"Rev. Dr. R——, of the reformed Presbyterian Church, has been deposed, on account of a crim. con. with a lady who resides at Pittsburg, Pa. The Dr. is 75 years of age, is a man of commanding appearance, and wears long silvery white hair; he has been married twice, his second wife has been for long time bedridden, and in one of his letters to Mrs.——, used as evidence against him, he mentioned the fact, said she was getting better, but it was not his fault. (The lady in question in the above case, is the widow of a clergyman, who is editress and proprietress of a monthly magazine, which is regarded as the organ of the American Scotch Covenanters)." One more:

"On Tuesday of last week, the sexton of Home Chapel, at Cleveland, Ohio, eloped with a young woman; he leaves a wife and seven children, and has heretofore been considered a pattern of piety and morality."—*Cleveland Herald, June* 1, 1859. Still another, a later occurrence.

"The Rev. Dr. Pomeroy, a Boston divine of most *Orthodox* pretentions, who has for years filled a position of the highest honor and trust in the gift of his brethren, (Sec. Board of Foreign Missions) has been detected in immoral practices, which have been for a long time kept from public exposure, only by a liberal application of hush money.

The Boston Journal, from which we take the above, says, in comment, sanctimoniously :

"Whatever Dr. Pomeroy may be guilty of, no discredit is to be attached to his denomination or the Society of which he was a prominent officer,"—refreshing, truly. This list might also be extended indefinitely, but we will now leave these sects, and turn to the Methodists, a few moments :

This is the most numerous and pretentious sect in this country, unlike the spiritual Wesley, their founder, who looked above for strength and guidance, and acknowledged spirit communion. (See Murray's Life of Wesley.) Their religion is of an earthly nature, appealing to the lower or subordinate faculties of mind, morbid sympathy, fear, revenge, undue reverence and sensitiveness, are the avenues through which they make converts. The writer of these pages has seen much of their efforts in this department, has attended camp meeting where thousands were assembled, and hundreds groaning, bellowing, rolling on the ground, climbing tent poles, and falling down with the power, besides a great many other performances, too ridiculous and indecent to put in print; and all in the name of religion. The manner of their preaching, too, shows that they rely on these excitements for the evidence of real conversion, the preachers seldom speak of what they know, or strive by reason to reach their hearers; but 'tis what they *feel*, and have *felt*, that forms the principal part of their exhortations. This shows that theirs is a religion of feeling and sensation, not reason. This is all the reason we can give for the negros generally being Methodists, and the large class of small intellects that you will always see taking a very active part at camp meetings and revivals. There are some good men, intelligent people, among this sect, but it is generally admitted by disinterested critics, that the majority of them are of the class just alluded to. Well, we are glad there is a Methodist church for them to go to; they would be out of their place anywhere else. Such classes of people, mingling together promiscuously, as in camp meetings, and other such gatherings, is admirably calculated to develope practical freeloveism, and this is the only way we can account for there being a greater number of cases of immorality in this, than in any other denomination. We have within our reach at this time, over a hundred, which have occurred among Methodist ministers alone, in the last two years, but a few of which we shall insert here. First, we would say, we know of no denomination more bitter against all reformers, spiritualists, etc., accusing them of almost unheard of immoralities, without a particle of proof. Many of their leading divines, to our certain knowledge, have lied more about that class of people, than ever the Jesuits did about their direst enemies; and if their secret by-laws could be read, (judging from their words and deeds) they would go something like the following: " Lying is no sin under *any* circumstances, provided the lie thus told is about a spiritualist, or for the interest of the church in any way whatever." Let these revilers look back to some of the highest lights in their own Church.

Let us call to their remembrance one E. K. Avery, one of the greatest camp meeting revivalists ever known, who flourished in the New England States some 25 years ago; who seduced, and then murdered the unfortunate victim of his passions; though a tricky tribunal let him go without condign punishment, public opinion then and now has most loudly and universally condemned him. Likewise the eloquent Maffit, whose converts were numbered by thousands, in all the principal cities in this country, could also be traced by his intrigues in every place where he preached. He was married several times, and his seductions were too numerous to mention. We have the following anecdote of his *loving* propensity from an eye witness :

He was preaching one evening in a southern city, where he was getting up a revival, and walking the aisles with fervor, as was his wont, when he spied a surpassingly beautiful young lady in tears; he spoke to her, asked her if she loved Jesus ? she replied, sobbing, that she hoped she did. Well then, said he quickly, kiss me for *Christ's* sake; and she kissed him." Suppose some spiritual lecturer should conduct himself in that way; every methodist preacher who could boast half a horse power, would preach a sermon on the demoralizing tendency of spiritualism. But to come down to the newspapers of the present year, we find the following case of adultery and murder :

"Rev. Mr. ——, of Montgomery Co. Ind., was arrested in Detroit on Monday last, (Dec. 2, 1858) charged with having poisoned his wife. He is about fifty years of age, *and has for a long time been a member of the Methodist Church*, sustaining a high character in community. The woman whose death he is charged with causing, was his second wife; she died very suddenly, having been in perfect health the day previous. Remarks of his at the time of her burial caused suspicion, and her body was taken up for examination, when the wretch fled. A large quantity of strychnine was found in her stomach. His first wife who died very suddenly fifteen years ago, is now believed to have been poisoned. The incentive to this crime, was an improper intimacy with a young woman."—Detroit Paper of above date.

Another. "A Double Elopement.—A Methodist local preacher has eloped from Elk River, Va., with two daughters of one Michael Griffith, leaving a wife and large family in destitute circumstances."—N. Y. Herald. Again: "A man about fifty years of age, a Methodist Minister of Brown Co. Ind., came to Richmond, Ind., a short time since, in company with a young lady apparently about seventeen years of age, and put up at a private boarding house, where the young lady gave birth to a child; this child was afterward murdered, and the guilty pair were arrested and committed to jail."—Dayton, O., Paper. This list could also be extended a hundred pages, but we forbear. We have omitted names in most of the above instances, because our aim is *not to give currency to scandal*, as some might suppose, but to point a moral, which will appear in conclusion, viz :—to show that these men, who make such great pretentions are only human, and these religious creeds, instead of promoting morality, are directly the opposite in their tendency, for this reason : they found their religion on the false idea that man is totally depraved by nature, a subject of wrath, and child of the devil. Now every one knows, in the common affairs of life, give a man a poor opinion of his own powers in any department of life, and it hinders his success therein; no matter whether it is in business life, social ethics, politics or religion. So with man as a whole being, if he thinks he is totally depraved, that very idea leads him to conclusions like this: "well, I am depraved any way, so it makes no odds what I do; then, after a while, perhaps, he becomes converted, his faith is strong, he believes that by it alone he is to be saved, he is taught by his religion that good works are unavailing, so he will say to himself, (if naturally inclined to sensuality or crime,) "it makes no difference what I do, I believe and have faith, and am therefore bound to be saved, let me behave ever so bad, (only don't let me loose my faith). So he has nothing to keep him from excess, debauchery and crime. We blame them not, nor would we reproach them, though necessity compels us to state unpleasant facts. They must fulfil their circle in that condition of animality, ere they can rise to a more exalted condition. We even admit all these forms, degrading as they appear to be, necessary; they have filled a place naught else could fill, but they are not final. There are, no doubt, a large number on earth who need creeds and ceremonies, also, there may be those who need that very sensual life which we despise, but there are many who have progressed above them all, and look back upon them as an olden garment of no further use, being worn out and full of holes, no more competent to clothe the immortal spirit. Oh! when will these bigots learn that they cannot force full grown men into the swaddling clothes of infants, or cast the soul that has once tasted of freedom, back into the rusty shackles of former ages. This lesson must be learned sooner or later, and these proud creed-men shown the strength of the mighty power that is now assisting in this great work of spiritual improvement. They are even now beginning to feel the power of the genius of religious progress, and list to those angel voices that tell of a brighter world beyond the grave, and a purer religion for man on earth. They, many of them, mourn over the rapid strides of the "New Religion," and the daily deterioration of Church influence. The struggle is hard; they hate to give up the power they have wielded for ages; but if their spiritual vision could be opened, and they behold the myriads of the wise departed who are battling on the side of truth and freedom, they would shrink with dismay to their cloisters, and no more strive to war against fate.

CHAPTER VII.

SPIRITUALISM—ITS MEDIUMS AND BELIEVERS—ITS EFFECT ON THEIR MORALS—ITS EFFECT ON THE OPPOSING WORLD—CONCLUSION.

The advent of modern spiritualism, its commencement with the simple raps, its continued increase in quantity, and diversity of quality of manifestations, are all well known facts, admitted by the public, whether they receive the ida of their spiritual origin or not. That there are manifestations that profess to be spiritual, is a well known fact. Not only this, but the believers in the Philosophy and religion of spiritualism are now numbered by millions, and its mediums by thousands, in this country alone, besides a great many in Europe, and other places in the old world. We have not room in this short chapter to enter into a lengthy argument to prove the reality of spiritual intercourse, nor is it necessary. We only wish to enquire into its effects on the morals of those who receive it as a heaven-born truth. All religious denominations admit that man has within him a *something* that lives after the body is dead, though none of them are able to define it, or tell aught definitely concerning it; nothing about its shape here, the part of the body it occupies, or the form it bears after it leaves the body; yet they are continually talking about saving the soul. Spiritualism tells man what his soul is, then shows him how to save it, by bringing to his presence the realities of the future life, which is but a continuation of this. The more exalted the mind in this, the higher the station it will take in the next state of existence. This gives man an incentive to progress here, and an object to live for, inasmuch as it makes practical goodness the only basis of happiness, either here or hereafter. It shows human life to be spiral in its course onward and upward, like all material forms below it on earth. Man commences his existence here, an infant; this may be illustrated by taking a coil of wire, shaped like a cone, invert it and call the pointed end infancy; as the human being grows to manhood its sphere of observation enlarges; as you continue to trace the wire, you find as you advance, that with every step toward the larger end, it increases in size. So with the different steps of mental growth, as the mind advances a step higher in refinement, civilization and goodness, its sphere of observation enlarges, and the greater room there is for still higher attainment. The growth and progress of the human spirit is like a cone formed wire, tha- hrs no end, and when the spirit "shuffles off this mortal coil," it goes forth into another school of life with the a, b, c, it has learned in this, the primary school of eternity, to that principal sshool, where the letters are to be formed into words, sentences, and realities of eternal existence; and inasmuch as the mind, which is the real man, loses nothing by passing through the change called death, it still has the desire to commune with the friends it has left behind, and still feels an interest in their welfare: hence spirit communion. Now most religious sects believe there was a time when spirits returned to earth, (their sacred writings are full of such instances) but they say the day of such revelations has passed away; though that same book says: "God is unchangeable, and his laws immutable, the same yesterday, to-day and forever." So, if there was a law by which a spirit could communicate, eighteen hundred or four thousand years ago, that same law is in full force to-day. Again, there is not to be found between the lids of the Bible, a single sentence, that can even be distorted into saying: "after a certain time spirits shall no more return to earth, and the gates of inspiration be forever closed." On the contrary, a host of passages can be found, that convey the idea very distinctly that such things shall continue. "I will send you the comforter, the Holy Ghost, which is the spirit of truth, and he shall abide with you forever."—Jesus. "Follow after charity and *desire spiritual* gifts."—Paul. "But you have a more sure word of prophesy, unto which you do well to take heed, *until the day dawns, and the day star arise in your heart.*"—Peter. "And I saw a new heaven, and a new earth, for the former had passed away; and I saw the holy city, the New Jerusalem, coming down out of heaven as a bride adorned for her husband, etc.' Jno. So it seems all these writers whom we quote, looked forward to a time when the minds of earth would be more spiritual, and have the "day star" shed its divine radiance within their souls. This, in their view, was to be brought about by spiritual agencies. All religious sects now, we presume will agree with us, that it is the want of true spirituality, that is the cause of so much sensuality, crime and wickedness on earth at the present time; if so, then that which has a tendency to make man love sensual things less, and spiritual more, is what is most needed by humankind all over the world. We would then ask how can this state of things be bro't about? And various answers are given. Some say by the gospel, others by a greater amount of faith, or more strenuous laws to regulate the *opinions* of men; others, one idea men, say by the abolition of slavery, or war, by communism, or a different system of trade. We will not stop here to discuss the beauty or deformity of these several ideas advocated so zealously by many honest people, but simply inquire, do they reach the root of the matter? By no means. There is something deeper still, needed to strike the key note of the human soul, and cause it to vibrate to the harmony of true goodness, and angelic purity. Man is a spiritual being, he needs *spiritual culture;* the Church cannot satisfy all his wants in this department; the worm-eaten theologies of former ages fail to meet this hunger and thirst after spiritual food. The creeds of man seem to the aspiring spirit, like the husk which tells of the ripe corn not yet attained. Spiritualism is the ripened ear of grain, which to the hungry soul, comes as manna to support it, while in the wilderness of doubt and uncertainty, which has ever seemed to shroud the human spirit in its earthly pilgrimage. Paul commanded the Corinthians, to "desire spiritual gifts" —1st Cor. 14-1. after enumerating the various gifts in detail, viz:— "The gift of healing, speaking with tongues, discerning spirits, prophesy, etc." (see 1st Cor. 12.) Now if these gifts were to be so useful to the Corinthians, why should not we, Americans, desire the same gifts? The mediums of this age have these gifts? The number of the sick that have been healed by these influences, if all their names were printed, would fill a dozen such pamphlets as this; there is scarce a town, village or neighborhood, in this country, in which some such cases have not transpired. The gift of speaking with tongues, or in other languages than their own, is a very common thing among mediums; we know personally more than a thousand who have thus spoken or written under spiritual control, languages of which they were themselves entirely ignorant. The writer of these pages has thus spoken and written nine different languages, and is acquainted in his normal condition with but three. "Of discerning spirits." This gift is a very common one among mediums; many there are who daily see and converse with their spirit friends. The gift of prophesy, also, whether you give it the modern definition, foretelling future events, or the Apostolic definition, speaking spiritual truths, both these gifts are certainly manifested by different mediums; and as well authenticated as anything can be by human testimony. These are a few of the facts on which spiritualists predicate their religion. We would ask any candid mind, if there is anything in the catalogue of gifts we have just enumerated, which is calculated to inculcate anything but the highest toned moral character? If one fully realizes that his angel mother or pure-hearted sister, is watching over him from the land of spirits, how can he but be elevated by such knowledge and such heavenly guardianship! he must indeed be very low and degraded who would not feel holy emotions and exalted aspirations, under such heavenly guidance. Mediums in particular, have an influence around them, which is calculated to assist them in their battle of life, quicken their aspirations, and lead them to look continually for instruction from the spiritual world. Let us not be misunderstood. We do not assert that *all* spiritualists and mediums are perfect; not so, for all sorts of people have friends in the other world, and inasmuch as every one enters the next life just as he leaves this, and like attracts like is a law of nature, there will be all kinds of control manifested, good, bad and indifferent; and as long as so many liars, deceivers, bigots, sensualists, and debauchees leave this world for the other, is it to be wondered at that some of them occasionally come back *seeking their affinities*. But take the spiritual influences and communications as a whole, that have been in the last eleven years poured forth through undeveloped mediums, and under necessarily adverse circumstances, and any candid mind will find that it is calculated to enhance rather than to retard human progress, to give more truth than error, virtue than vice. It is but a child of eleven years of age, and if the child can do so much, what must the man be capable of? or in other words, if the spirits, laboring under these unfavorable influences, obliged to meet the prejudices of skeptics, the chicanery of bigots, and the pious lies of a creed-bound clergy, and a people submissive to their will; besides all the fears of ghosts, gouls and devils, which have been inculcated in the minds of most of the present generation from their earliest years; if they can lead millions to know of immortality, and the continual presence of their spirit friends —cause so many sick to be healed, and such a multitude of minds to be convinced of these heaven-born truths in the first eleven years, what may we not look forward to, that is exalted and powerful, as sure to take place in the same number of years to come? doubtless the most sanguine among us, can have but a faint idea. What is it that makes the Christian Church, as a body, so opposed to these modern revelations? Is it because they really believe that the gifts we have spoken of have a tendency to make people worse, more immoral and criminal? We cannot believe that any, except the most ignorant, or at least those who are most ignorant of what spiritualism really is, are so blind as to suppose that what made the ancient Hebrew Seers and Prophets and the Apostles filled with truth from on high, can make us moderns fiends incarnate. The majority of them *do not oppose* spiritualism for this reason, but because these spirits, as a general thing, teaches a religion broader, more comprehensive and more practical than that which they advocate; and they see that the moment they become believers in spirit communion, they will of course look more to the living gospel of to-day, and less to the belief of bygone ages. Here then, is the root of our offending; we dare to assert that their dogmas are not final, while we admit they have been useful in their place. This is the reason why the clergy are so bitter in their denunciations of all believers in spiritualism, and mediums in particular. They see that if spiritualism continues to increase the number of its follows they will in time be supplanted, and their places taken by others, by these very mediums whom they have despised and hated; for many of the disciples of the New Religion, are like those of Jesus of old, taken from the lower ranks of society, (as the world reckons.) This is the reason why evangelical divines, will, with such extreme unction, tell string after string of the sheerest fabrications, about naked circles, freeloving spiritualists, etc., without any care as to who may suffer from their falsehoods, and to their shame be it spoken, many of them have relatives whom they honor and respect, who are firm spiritualists, thereby showing their falsehood and baseness in its most deplorable light. We have heard a learned divine, a bright light in the Methodist Church, dilate for an hour or more on the damning wickedness and immorality of all Spiritualists, whose aged father, a man ten times as intelligent as his recreant son, is a pious Spiritualist—more than that, a man whose character had never been called in question. What can you call this except downright falsehood, and the most transparent dishonesty. A well known Baptist Divine in P———, in this State, asserted in a sermon, that *he knew* of a place in that vicinity, where spiritualists, male and female, held circles in a state of nudity! and when challenged by a gentleman who was there, to produce the proof and tell where the place was, he declined; moreover, this same person made the Rev. a proposal as follows: He, the divine, should have as much time as he pleased, and be allowed to find every case of immorality, that had ever occurred among the Spiritualists of Michigan, and his opponent would guarantee to find more cases of a like character, in the same length of time, in that County alone, *in the Baptist Church. This offer was also declined.* This is the course taken by all public opponents of spiritualism we have ever met, and their name is legion; we have yet to hear a single one, priest or layman, that did not use low slang and blackguardism; and assail the character of spiritualists and mediums. All of these facts show plainly that they cannot make a straight forward, manly argument against them. Great men have tried it and failed. But they can pour forth their billingsgate in the name of religion, and it will be taken for gospel truth by some, who have not strength of mind enough to break from the leading strings of blind faith inculcated by a designing priesthood. Spiritualists all court discussion and investigation, they care not how close people are in their search provided they will be honest, and admit the truth when it is made plainly manifest; but when we see these pretentious divines, Professors and other men who know better, showing such a palpable lack of candor and fairness we can but come to the above conclusion, and think that they also see the hopelessness of their success, and their terrible opposition is but the last struggle against fate. Spiritualism inculcates morality, and is to man a practical good. First, because it demonstrates to him the immortality of the soul, and reveals to him some of the realities of the future life, and takes from him that dread of death which has for ages shrouded the human spirit with gloom, doubt and fear. Second: It reveals the law of Progress in all its glorious beauty, and tells that life is progressive. Third: It makes practical righteousness the only basis of happiness. When you tell an individual that he can go right to the arms of Jesus on the strength of faith, you take away all incentive to an upright and moral life, besides, it is one of the greatest pieces of injustice, to make faith or belief, (neither of which come voluntarily, but by force of evidence,) the promise of happiness, or the lack of it a passport to eternal woe. To illustrate, suppose one of the lowest and most debased specimens of humanity on earth, should go by night to the bedside of an upright, honest, moral man, (not a believer in theology,) and in cool blood plunge the dagger into the heart of his sleeping victim; according to *evangelical* theology, that upright, virtuous man would go direct to the infernal regions for lack of faith. After proper time, the guilty wretch who did the deed, is brought to trial and condemned to death, before his execution the priests gather round him, talking, praying, etc., he has a change of heart and is baptised ; then this black-hearted murderer, his hands wreaking with his brother's blood, is launched into heaven; from the gallows direct to the arms of Jesus, while the innocent murdered is weltering in the flames of hell. Can the human imagination conceive of a blacker piece of injustice than this? Still, this is a fair picture of what would necessarily be, if orthodox theology was true. On the other hand, spiritualism says, the next life being but a continuanion of this these two men who thus suddenly entered there, would take places suited to their condition ; the pure hearted man thus stricken by the assassin's hand, would enter a sphere where he would associate with those of like character and tastes to himself ; and the other, the guilty murderer, would enter one of the lower states, there to be taught the lesson of purity and goodness the other had learned on earth. Which of these two theories is best calculated to lessen crime, and make mankind more moral and virtuous? Why, evidently, that which says, no reward except for goodness, no forgiveness of sins, no atonement, except by practical righteousness. Here, then, is the Spiritual standard, "Faith, without works, is dead, being alone. Show us your faith without your works, and we will show ours by our works." And again, we would say to our opposers, in the language of the same apostle James, "When will ye know, O vain man, that faith without works is dead?" Fourth, Spiritual intercourse makes people happier. Happiness is the chief end of all human hopes, the reward of all aspirations, then whatever enhances the happiness of mankind most, is what they most need ; is it not a pleasure to know, that those whom you have mourned as dead still live, and are with you still?

Is there not something exalting in such a knowledge? Then again, the religion taught has a tendency to give man confidence in himself, in nature, and nature's God ; he looks upon himself as a progressive being, not dependent upon the goodness of another, for his happiness here or in the future life, knowing that it will be *his own goodness*, or the lack of it, that will make him happy, or miserable; that the soul contains within itself, its recompense for good or ill, its own hereafter, Redeemer and Judge. With such a knowledge, he can look forth to Deity as the Father and Mother of the Universe, pervading all things, and working all things together for the good of the whole; and each component part, man included, who is the highest specimen of Divinity we, as finite beings, can ever behold, or contemplate, man on earth and man in the spirit world. Here we learn this great lesson, to love God, by living and serving humanity; thereby making our own happiness sure by striving to learn that beautiful lesson, taught by Spirits and re-echoed throughout the material universe, "Learn to make others happy."

We have now given a few of our reasons why the religion of Spiritualism teaches a higher morality than any other. We would also say, for the benefit of those who are not familiar with this new religion, that it has no articles of faith, no written creed, nor does it need any, for it is by nature written in some degree in every human soul, where the deep welling waters of aspiration are ever gushing forth, mingled in some degree, with that Spiritual fountain whose waters are never quenched. When the truth of Spiritualism is fully realized, it is not a *faith*, nor yet a *belief*, but a *knowledge*, that can never be taken away. There are four points on which all Spiritualists agree, however much they may differ in things which are mere matters of opinion, viz: Existence of Deity, Immortality of the Soul, Eternal Progress, and Spiritual Intercourse. In these four short sentences there is embodied thought enough for a life time, opening wide the gateways of knowledge, and proclaiming to man his future destiny. It is a rule in nature, that a person, power or principle, cannot bestow that which it does not or has not possessed. We have shown, we think satisfactorily, that this religion *does not* contain within itself a single germ of immorality; consequently, if any of its followers have given way to human weakness, it is not their religion that has made them sin, or that justifies them in their iniquity, for let them have ever so much faith, be ever so sorry, and shed ever so many tears, it is of no avail; their religion tells them they must take the consequences of their own misdeeds, and wipe out the stain by turning from iniquity and wrong, to purity and goodness. But most of the awful stories about the wickedness of mediums, &c., that find their way into the public prints, have not the slightest foundations in fact. All this twaddle about naked circles, freelove gatherings, &c., is, to our certain knowledge, the sheerest fabrication. We have been in almost every State of the Union, and it has been our lot and pleasure to mingle much with all classes of people, and among Spiritualists especially, for the last five years, and we find fewer cases of *alleged* immorality among Spiritualists than in any other religious denomination. The facts, thus far, corroborate our axioms before stated. To ourself, as an individual, Spiritualism is a Heavenly truth, a holy religion, a savor of life unto life, from error, infidelity and false theology, to a realization of our eternal existence, and the continued presence of the loved departed, who have gone before us to that brighter world. We would say, in conclusion, that there never has been a time so auspicious for Spiritualism and its followers, as the present. The genius of Spiritual freedom seems bending its pinions still nearer to earth, than ever before; mediums are increasing daily, and the number of *anxious inquirers*, was never before so numerous as now. Then let us all strive daily and hourly to draw still nearer to those angel guides, and strive with them for the devotion and spiritualization of humanity. Let bigots sneer, and scoffers scoff, heed them not, save to battle continually for the right, ever bearing in mind, 'that those that are for us, are more than those that are against us

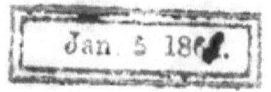

www.ingramcontent.com/pod-product-compliance
Lightning Source LLC
Chambersburg PA
CBHW032240080426
42735CB00008B/936